TO ACCOMPANY

AIR PILOT'S MANUAL - VOLUME 3

Questions, Answers & Explanations

EASA PPL Revision Papers

Navigation

Written and illustrated by

Helena B A Hughes

POOLEY'S

Air Pilot Publishing

Nothing in this manual supersedes any EU legislation, rules or EASA regulations or procedures and any operational documents issued by The Stationery Office, the Civil Aviation Authority, National Aviation Authorities, the manufacturers of aircraft, engines and systems, or by the operators of aircraft throughout the world. Note that as maps and charts are changed regularly, those extracts reproduced in this book must not be used for flight planning or flight operations.

EASA Private Pilot Licence Aeroplane & Helicopter Questions, Answers & Explanations – Navigation

ISBN 978-1-84336-211-1

First Edition published March 2014
Reprinted June 2014
Second Edition December 2015

Origination by Pooleys Flight Equipment Limited.

Published by Pooleys Flight Equipment Ltd

Elstree Aerodrome
Hertfordshire WD6 3AW
Tel: +44(0)20 8953 4870
Web: www.pooleys.com
Email: sales@pooleys.com

AUTHOR

Helena B A Hughes

Helena Hughes was born into an aviation household, having her first informal "flying lesson" at the age of four. Her late father David was a flying instructor and also flew corporate jets. On leaving University Helena obtained her PPL. Shortly afterwards she started work in Air Traffic Control at London Luton Airport earning her Controllers Licence in 1990. Helena continues to be an operational Air Traffic Control Officer and is currently posted to Swanwick working "Thames Radar", "Luton Radar" and "Heathrow Special"; she is involved in controller training as both an Instructor and Assessor. Helena holds a fixed wing CPL/IR and has been a flying instructor since 1996. She also holds a PPL(H) and is a Radio Telephony and Air/Ground Examiner.

Helena would like to thank: Mrs. Brenda "Bedda" Hughes; Mr. Andrew Temple of Solent Flight Ltd; A Vrancken and H Ewing

INTRODUCTION

This book is intended as an aid to revision and examination preparation for those studying for the grant of an EASA PPL. Ideally its use should follow a period of self or directed study to consolidate the knowledge acquired and identify any areas of weakness prior to attempting the PPL examinations themselves.

The questions and answers in this publication are designed to reflect those appearing in the current examination papers and are set out in a representative format. No attempt has been made to replicate any actual examination paper.

Blank answer sheets are provided at the end of the book which may be photocopied to enable multiple attempts at each exam.

EDITORS

Dorothy Saul-Pooley LLB(Hons) FRAeS

Dorothy holds an ATPL (A) and a CPL (H), and is both an instructor and examiner on aeroplanes and an instructor on helicopters. She is Head of Training for a school dedicated to running Flight Instructor courses at Shoreham. She is also a CAA Flight Instructor Examiner. In addition, having qualified as a solicitor in 1982, Dorothy acted for many years as a consultant specialising in aviation and insurance liability issues, and has lectured widely on air law and insurance issues. This highly unusual combination of qualifications led to her appointment as Honorary Solicitor to the Guild of Air Pilots and Navigators (GAPAN). Dorothy is a Fellow of the Royal Aeronautical Society, first Chairman of the GAPAN Instructor Committee, and past Chairman of the Education & Training Committee. She has just completed her term of office as the Master for the year 2014-15 of the Honourable Company of Air Pilots (formerly GAPAN). She is also Chairman of the Professional Flying Instructors Association. In 2003 she was awarded the Jean Lennox Bird Trophy for her contribution to aviation and support of Women in Aviation and the BWPA (British Women Pilots Association). In 2013 Dorothy was awarded the prestigious Master Air Pilots Certificate by GAPAN. A regular contributor to seminars, conferences and aviation publications. Dorothy is the author and editor of a number of flying training books and has published articles in legal and insurance journals.

Daljeet Gill BA(Hons)

Daljeet is the Head of Design & Development for Pooleys Flight Equipment and editor of the Air Pilot's Manuals, Guides to the EASA IR & CPL Flight Test, Pre-flight Briefing and R/T Communications as well as many other publications. Daljeet has been involved with the editing, typesetting and designing of all Pooleys publications and products since she joined us in 2001. Graduating in 1999 with a BA(Hons) in Graphic Design, she deals with marketing, advertising, exhibition design and technical design of our manufactured products in the UK. She maintains our website and produces our Pooleys Catalogue. Daljeet's design skills and imaginative approach have brought a new level of clarity and readability to the projects she has touched.

EASA PRIVATE PILOT LICENCE
- AEROPLANE -
NAVIGATION

Before attempting these practice examination papers, you should have read Air Pilot's Manual, Volume 3 – Navigation and have completed the Progress Tests at the end of that manual.

The Navigation examination consists of 19 questions; the time allowed is 1 hour and 15 minutes.

The pass mark is 75%.

Please read each question carefully and ensure you understand it fully before making your choice of answer.

Each question is multiple choice with four possible answers A, B, C and D. You should indicate your chosen answer by placing a cross in the appropriate box on the answer sheet.

Blank answer sheets are to be found at the end of this publication, these may be photocopied.

This section does not form part of the theoretical examination preparation, you will not be required to plot and plan a whole route. It is included to help you hone your navigation planning skills.

INTENTIONALLY BLANK

NAVIGATION PAPER 1

1. A VOR is a radio navigation aid that operates in which radio band?

a. MF
b. LF
c. UHF
d. VHF

2. The airborne VOR receiver:

a. Measures the range from the ground station. It measures the time taken for the interrogation pulse to return to the aircraft.
b. Measures the magnetic direction of the signal transmitted by the ground station.
c. Measures the true direction of the signal transmitted by the ground station.
d. Measures the phase difference between two signals transmitted by the VOR beacon.

3. A VOR radial is:

a. The true bearing from the station
b. The magnetic bearing from the station
c. The true bearing to the station
d. The magnetic bearing to the station

4. When flying towards a VOR on the 125 radial, in order to obtain CDI indications in the correct sense the OBS should be set to:

a. 125° with a FROM indication
b. 125° with a TO indication
c. 305° with a TO indication
d. 305° with a FROM indication

5. Which aircraft is on the 060° radial tracking towards a VOR beacon and receiving correct sense indications?

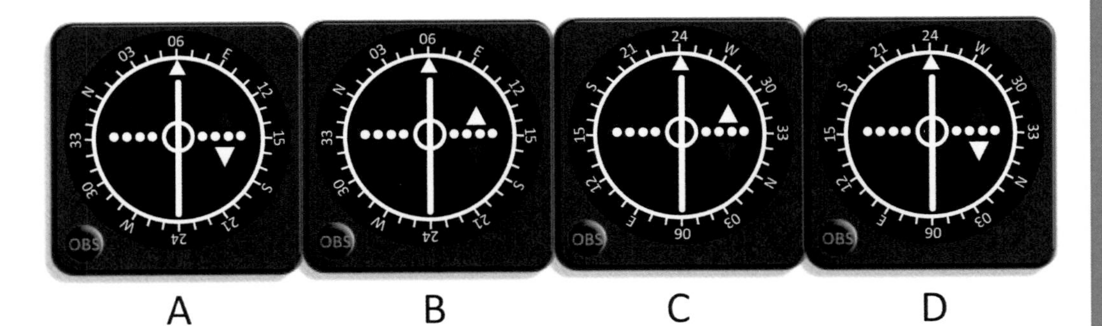

a. A
b. B
c. C
d. D

6. What is the name given to a line which crosses all meridians at the same angle?

a. A parallel
b. A great circle
c. A rhumb line
d. A grid line

7. A "Lambert" projection is best used for covering:

a. Mid-latitudes
b. Polar regions
c. Areas within 10° north or south of the equator
d. Areas with a great north/south extent

8. You are flying and maintaining a heading of 020° C with 5° right drift. From the compass card you know that the deviation is 3° E, the magnetic variation in the area is 4°W. What is the aircraft's true track?

a. 019° T
b. 026° T
c. 024° T
d. 014° T

9. If an aircraft flies due south along the 002° W meridian from latitude 53° 30′ N to 25° S. In nautical miles what distance is covered?

a. 4,680 nm
b. 4,710 nm
c. 1,710 nm
d. 4,650 nm

10. What is the meaning of the following symbols?

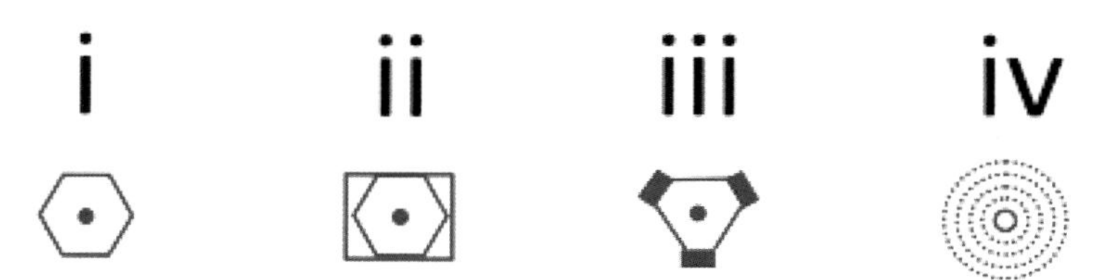

a.	i. TACAN	ii. VOR/DME	iii. VOR	iv. NDB
b.	i. VOR/DME	ii. TACAN	iii. NDB	iv. VOR
c.	i. VOR	ii. VOR/DME	iii. TACAN	iv. NDB
d.	i. VOR	ii. TACAN	iii. VOR/DME	iv. NDB

11. The angle between the Earth's magnetic field and the horizontal is referred to as:

a. Deviation
b. Variation
c. Slip (or "z")
d. Dip (or "z")

12. An aircraft is flying between two points 120 nm apart, after 40 nm the aircraft is found to be 5 nm to the right of track. In order to route directly to the destination what heading correction is necessary?

a. 7.5° left
b. 3.8° right
c. 11.2° left
d. 13.7° right

13. When using GPS, what is the minimum number of satellites required to provide three dimensional position fixing?

a. 4
b. 1
c. 2
d. 3

14. Overhead point A the fuel contents are 22 USG. 27 minutes later, over point B, the fuel contents is 17 USG. Your destination, C, is 55 minutes away.

Assuming the fuel flow remains constant and a Specific Gravity (Sp. G) of 0.72, how much fuel will remain, in kg, when overhead C?

a. 6.8 kg
b. 10.2 kg
c. 18.6 kg
d. 4.1 kg

15. An aircraft is flying at an indicated air speed (IAS) of 130 knots at FL 100. The OAT is +10° C, what is the aircraft's true airspeed (TAS)? Ignore position and instrument errors.

a. 150 kt
b. 134 kt
c. 162 kt
d. 156 kt

16. Complete the table below. From the completed table what is the magnetic heading and duration for the leg?

Pressure Altitude (FT)/ OAT(°C)	CAS (kt)	TAS (kt)	W/V	TR (T)	HDG (T)	Var.	HDG (M)	GS	DIST (NM)	Time
5000/+10	98		310/20	045		3W			56	

a. Magnetic Heading 037°; Duration 32 minutes
b. Magnetic Heading 034°; Duration 30 minutes
c. Magnetic Heading 031°; Duration 32 minutes
d. Magnetic Heading 034°; Duration 30 minutes

17. Given the following details calculate the wind velocity:

TAS	110 knots
GROUNDSPEED	96 knots
TRUE HEADING	165 degrees
TRUE TRACK	151 degrees

a. 040/20
b. 260/30
c. 170/35
d. 220/30

18. Your aircraft is maintaining a TAS of 102 knots and arrives overhead turning point A at 1030 UTC. Turning point B is 71 nm away using a track of 260° T. Calculate your ETA at B using a forecast wind of 310/15 kt.

a. 1108 UTC
b. 1131 UTC
c. 1117 UTC
d. 1125 UTC

19. Your destination is 80 nm away, you must arrive in not less than 50 minutes. If you are flying at FL 50 and the OAT is - 10° C. What is the minimum Calibrated Airspeed CAS required to arrive at the desired time?

Assume no head or tail wind component.

a. 96 kt
b. 89 kt
c. 91 kt
d. 102 kt

END OF NAVIGATION PAPER 1

INTENTIONALLY BLANK

NAVIGATION PAPER 1: ANSWERS

No	A	B	C	D
1				X
2				X
3		X		
4			X	
5			X	
6			X	
7	X			
8			X	
9		X		
10			X	
11				X
12			X	
13	X			
14			X	
15				X
16	X			
17				X
18			X	
19			X	

CORRECT ANSWERS: PERCENTAGES					
15	16	17	18	19	20
75%	80%	85%	90%	95%	100%

NAVIGATION PAPER 1: EXPLANATIONS

1. **(Answer: D)** The VOR operates in the VHF frequency band. VOR is an abbreviation for very high frequency omni-directional radio range. VORs are allocated frequencies between 108.0 MHz and 117.95 Mhz.

FURTHER READING: APM VOLUME 3, SECTION 4, CHAPTER 20 – THE VOR

2. **(Answer: D)** The VOR operates on the principle of phase comparison. The ground station transmits two VHF radio signals:

1. A reference signal: which is the same in all directions; and
2. A variable signal: the phase of this signal is made to vary at a constant rate throughout 360°.

The phase difference – the difference between the peaks of the radio waves - experienced by the receiver varies according to the aircraft's position around the station. When the aircraft is due north of the station the signals are in phase, i.e. they peak and trough at the same time.

The signals are then out of phase as follows:

090°M the signals are 90° out of phase
180°M the signals are 180° out of phase (anti-phase)
270°M the signals are 270° out of phase

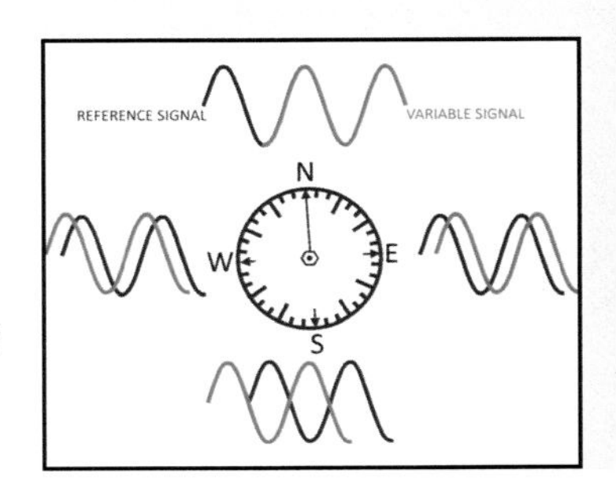

2. ANSWER D

Reference Signal (blue) and Variable Signal (red)

FURTHER READING: APM VOLUME 3, SECTION 4, CHAPTER 20 – THE VOR

3. **(Answer: B)** A VOR radial is the magnetic bearing from the station. A radial can also be thought of as a track away from a VOR beacon. The 360 tracks away from a VOR are separated from each other by 1° and are each related to magnetic north. A radial may also be called a QDR.

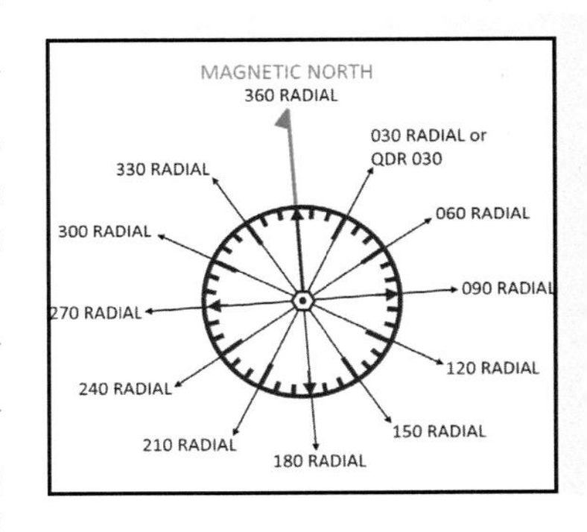

3. ANSWER B

A VOR Radial is the magnetic bearing from the station.

FURTHER READING: APM VOLUME 3, SECTION 4, CHAPTER 20 – THE VOR

4. **(Answer: C)** The cockpit display for the VOR is referred to as the OBS – omni bearing selector, it displays on a course card the radial selected by the pilot. The needle is referred to as the course deviation indicator, or CDI. If the aircraft is on the selected radial the needle will be in the centre. If it is not the needle will be deflected to the left or right as appropriate.

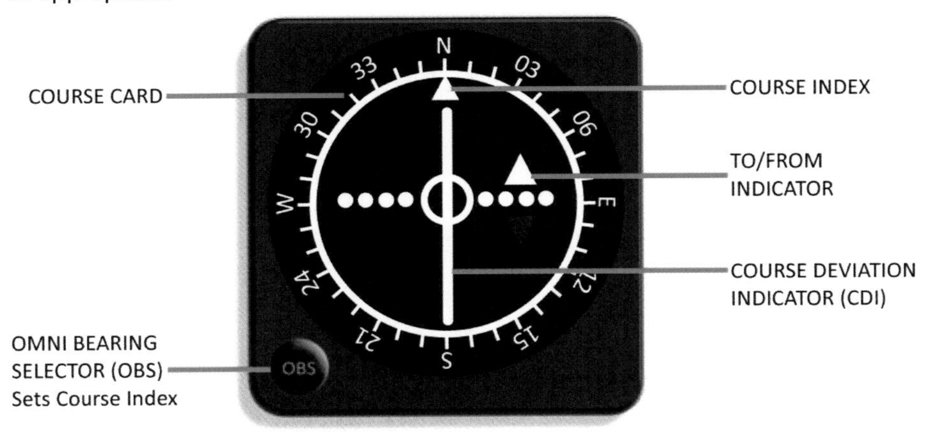

In this question we are told that the aircraft is on the 125 radial, i.e. it is to the south east of the beacon. In order to fly to the beacon with correct sense indications the OBS should be set to 305 with a TO indication.

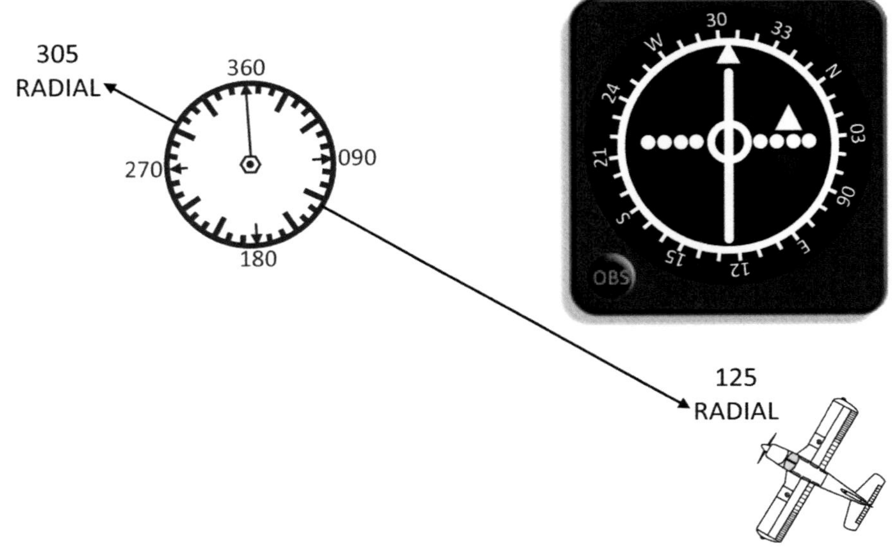

One way to think about the orientation is to remember that all the radio waves are emanating from the beacon and travelling away from it. For the OBS to work in the correct sense the TO/FROM indication should match the direction in which the selected radio wave is moving.

FURTHER READING: APM VOLUME 3, SECTION 4, CHAPTER 20 – THE VOR

5. **(Answer: C)** The radio waves are being emitted by the VOR beacon and moving away from it. In order to receive correct sense indications you need to be following a radial, or radio wave, travelling in the same direction as your aircraft. A TO indication shows that the selected course is on the other side of the VOR beacon. A FROM indication shows that the OBS selection and the aircraft are on the same side of the VOR.

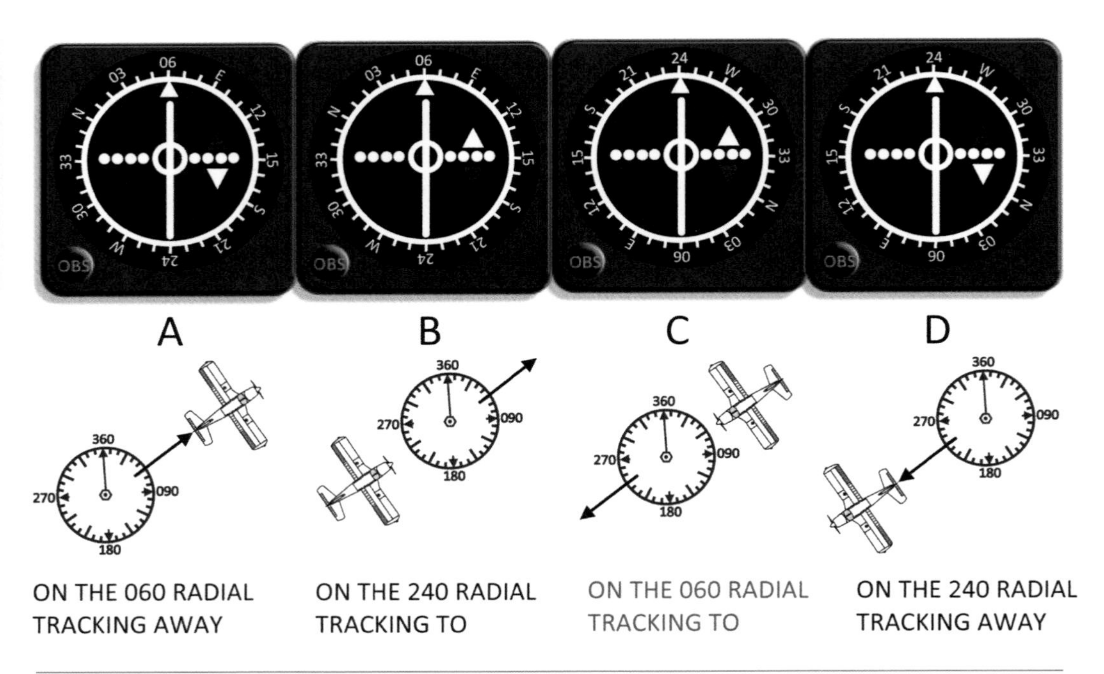

FURTHER READING: APM VOLUME 3, SECTION 4, CHAPTER 20 – THE VOR

6. **(Answer: C)** A rhumb line is a line which crosses all meridians of longitude at the same angle.

- A straight line drawn on a Transverse Mercator projection is a rhumb line.
- All parallels of latitude are rhumb lines, since they intersect with the meridians at the same angle.
- As a constant angle is maintained a rhumb line is easier to fly.

FURTHER READING: APM VOLUME 3, SECTION 1, CHAPTER 2 – AERONAUTICAL CHARTS

7. **(Answer: A)** "Lambert" projections are best suited to covering mid-latitude regions e.g. Europe, USA and Australia. At these latitudes the convergence of the meridians is not too extreme, as would be the case approaching the poles.

FURTHER READING: APM VOLUME 3, SECTION 1, CHAPTER 2 – AERONAUTICAL CHARTS

8. **(Answer: C)** The best way to begin with such questions is to use **T v M d C**, and to create a table containing the known details.

True Heading	Variation	Magnetic Heading	Deviation	Compass Heading
	4W		3E	020

Remember also "East is Least; West is Best" – meaning that easterly corrections are subtracted and westerly ones added **when working from left to right**. It is now possible to complete the table.

True Heading	Variation	Magnetic Heading	Deviation	Compass Heading
019	4W	**023**	3E	020
Check left to right: 019	*019+4*	*023*	*023-3*	*020*

The questions actually asks for the true track, not heading, and so now we must take into account the drift. Drift is measured from the heading (nose) to the track, and is classified in degrees port or starboard of heading.

The aircraft is heading 019° T with 5° of right (starboard) drift, therefore the true track is:

019 + 5 = 024° T

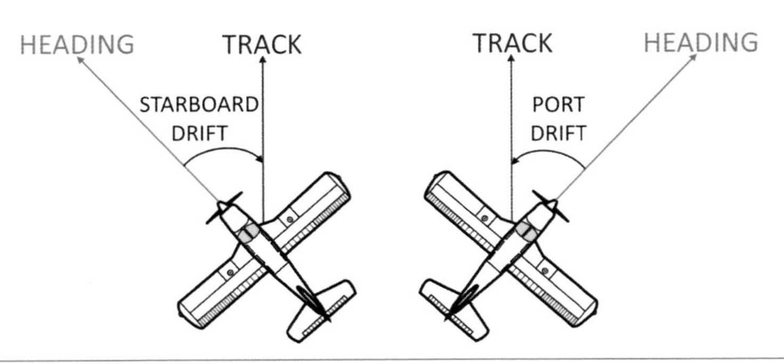

FURTHER READING: APM VOLUME 3, SECTION 1, CHAPTER 4 – THE MAGNETIC COMPASS AND DIRECTION

9. **(Answer: B)** A nautical mile is defined as a unit of distance equal to one minute (')of arc on the earth's surface. Each degree of latitude is made up of 60 minutes and therefore equates to 60 nm. As long as the movement is along a great circle, i.e. any meridian or the equator, the conversion between change in latitude and distance is straight forward.

To begin with find the total distance travelled in degrees and minutes. In this case the locations given are in opposite hemispheres and so the latitudes are added together: 53° 30' + 25 = 78° 30'

To find the distance in nm multiply each full degree travelled by 60: 78 x 60 = 4,680 nm

And add any extra minutes: 4,680 + (30 minutes at 1 nm per minute) = 4,710 nm

FURTHER READING: APM VOLUME 3, SECTION 2, CHAPTER 9 – DRIFT

10. **(Answer: C)**

VOR	VOR/DME	TACAN	NDB
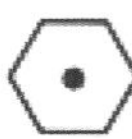	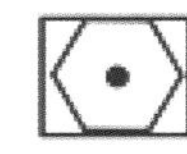	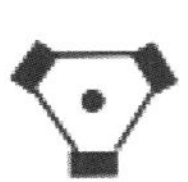	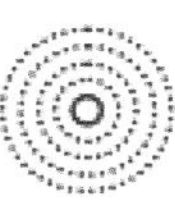

FURTHER READING: APM VOLUME 3, SECTION 1, CHAPTER 2 – AERONAUTICAL CHARTS

11. **(Answer: D)** Dip, or "z", is the angle between the Earth's magnetic field and the horizontal. Magnetic dip is caused by the magnets in a compass trying to align with the Earth's magnetic field which is practically horizontal at the equator, but almost vertical at the poles.

FURTHER READING: APM VOLUME 3, SECTION 1, CHAPTER 4 – THE MAGNETIC COMPASS AND DIRECTION

12. **(Answer: C)** 11.2° left. Off track errors can be calculated using the "One in Sixty" Rule.

TO FIND TRACK ERROR USING CRP

OUTER SCALE:	DISTANCE OFF TRACK (nm)	TRACK ERROR (degrees)
INNER SCALE:	DISTANCE TRAVELLED (nm)	60

TO FIND CLOSING ANGLE USING CRP

OUTER SCALE:	DISTANCE OFF TRACK (nm)	CLOSING ANGLE (degrees)
INNER SCALE:	DISTANCE TO GO (nm)	60

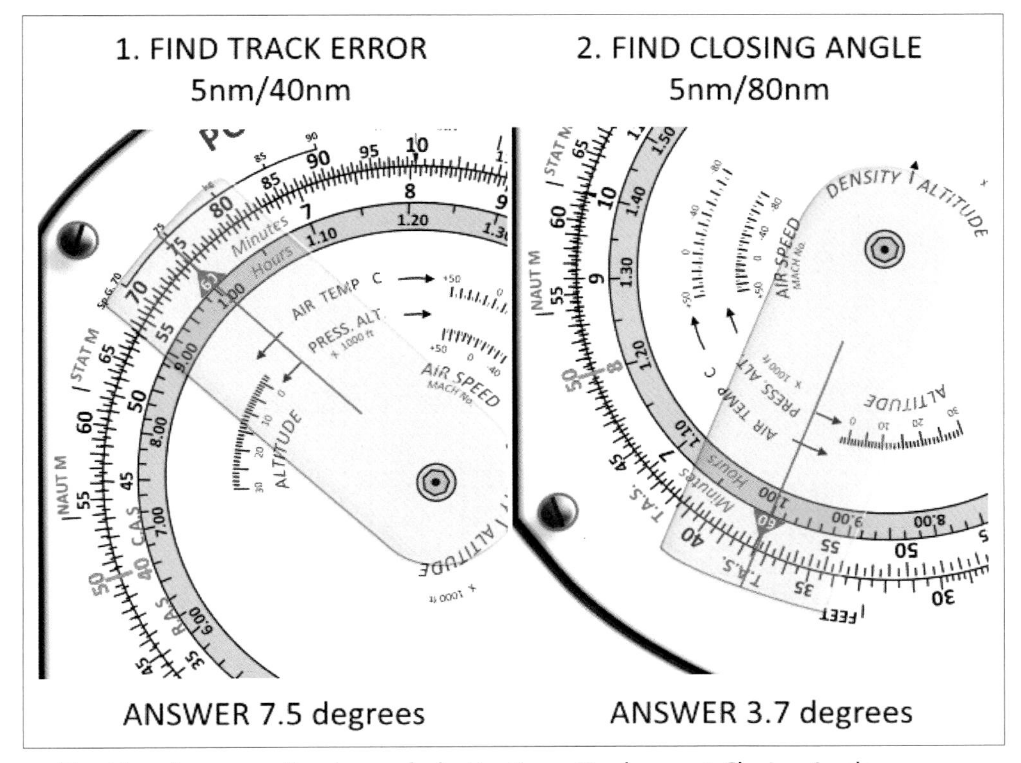

Total heading correction to reach destination = Track error + Closing Angle
= 7.5° + 3.7° = 11.2°
The heading must be corrected **11.2° left.**

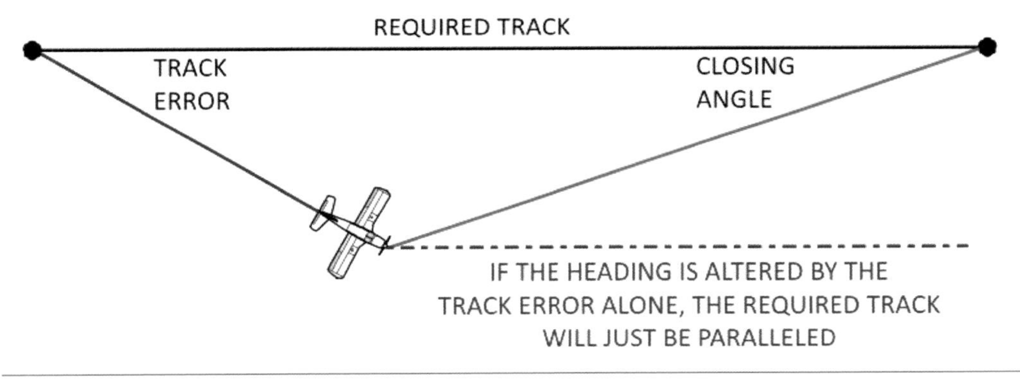

FURTHER READING: APM VOLUME 3, SECTION 3, CHAPTER 12 – ENROUTE NAVIGATION TECHNIQUES

13. **(Answer: A)** In order to calculate a three dimensional position a GPS receiver must be able to obtain signals from at least 4 satellites.

FURTHER READING: APM VOLUME 3, SECTION 4, CHAPTER 19 – GLOBAL POSITIONING SYSTEM (GPS)

14. (Answer: C) 18.6 kg.

Using the CRP-1 to find fuel consumption:

1. Set time elapsed between A and B, 27 minutes under the fuel used (22 –17 = 5 USG)
2. Read fuel consumption above the time index

Fuel flow 11.1 USG/hr

Outer Scale: Fuel Consumption	Fuel
Inner Scale: 60	Time

Fuel required to reach C:

3. Keep the CRP as it is, i.e with your calculated fuel consumption above the index
4. The next leg will take 55 minutes, find 55 on the inner rotating scale and read off

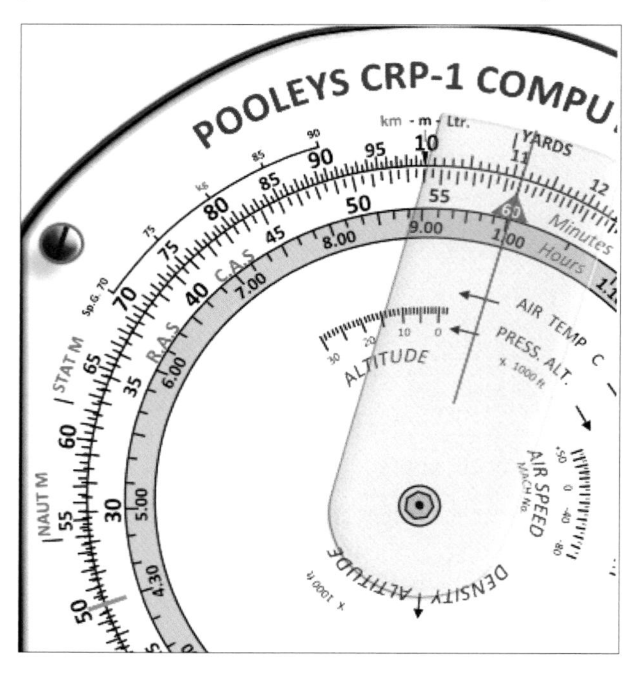

the fuel required above on the outer scale.

Fuel required: 10.2 USG. This answer is sensible, as 55 minutes is almost an hour. Therefore overhead C the remaining fuel will be: **17 – 10.2 = 6.8 USG**

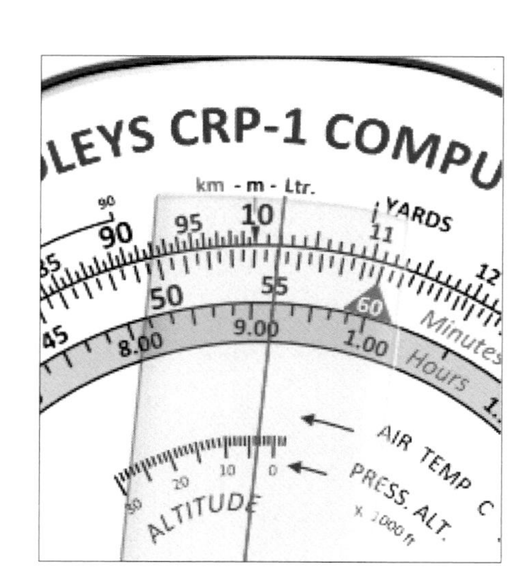

To find the weight of fuel in kg:

5. Set the amount of fuel, 6.8 USG, on the inner scale below the USG index
6. Set the guide line to the Sp.G scale for kg (be careful – there is a scale in lbs as well!)
7. Read off the weight in kg in the inner scale

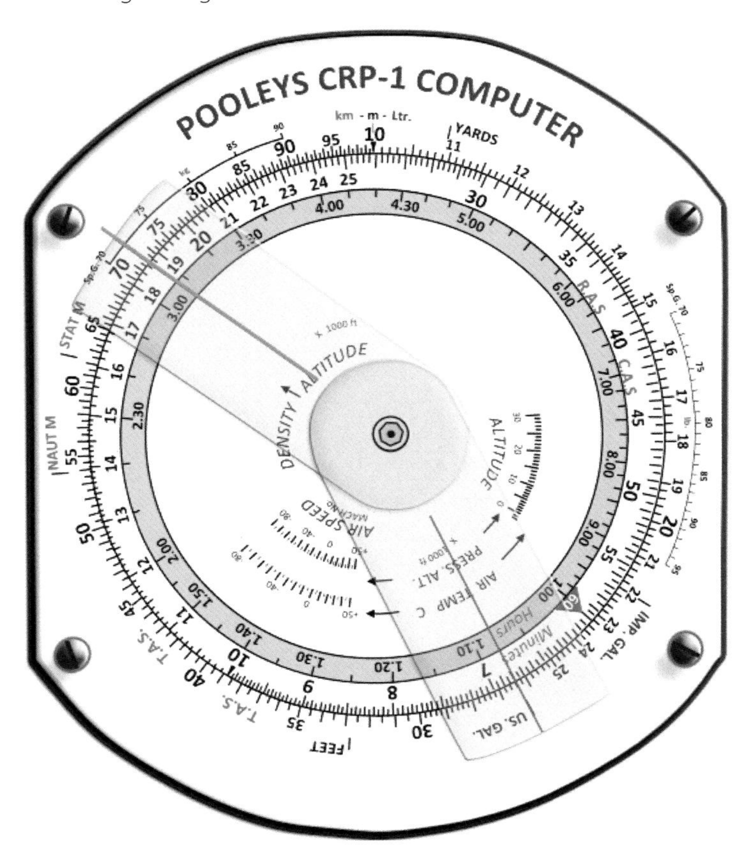

6.8 USG weighs 18.6 kg

FURTHER READING: APM VOLUME 3, SECTION 2, CHAPTER 10 – TIMING AND FUEL MANAGEMENT

15. (Answer: D) 156 knots.

1. In the AIRSPEED window, align the OAT with the pressure altitude

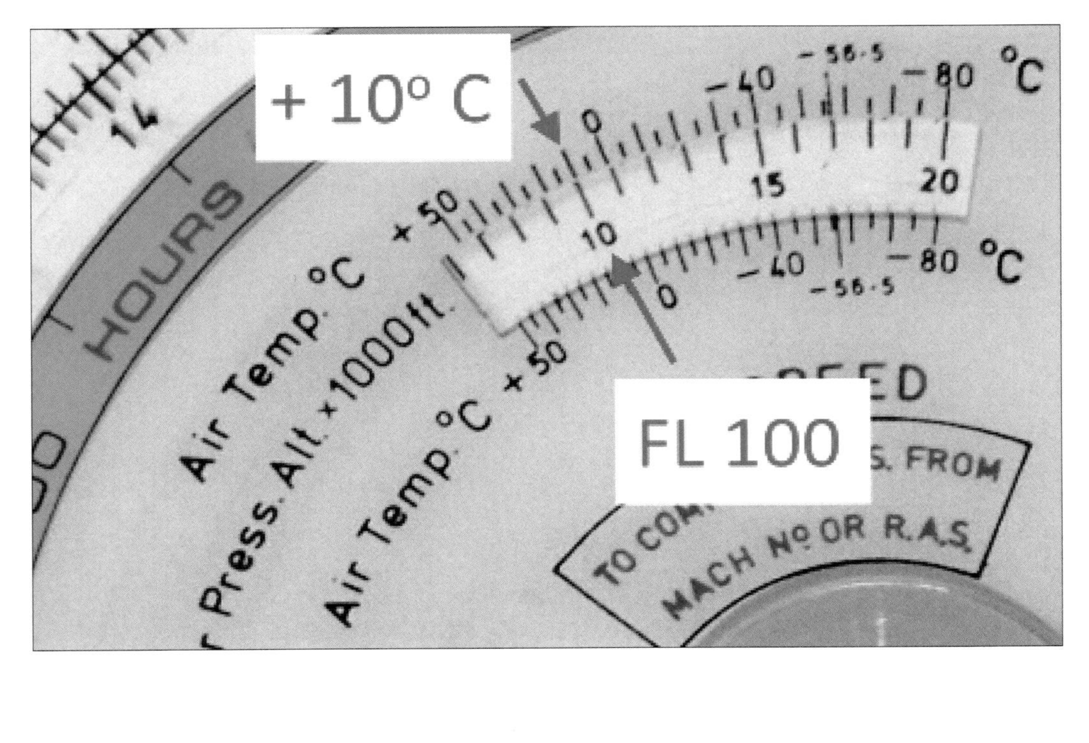

2. Find the IAS,130 kt, on the inner rotating scale. It is now possible to read off the TAS on the outer scale above.

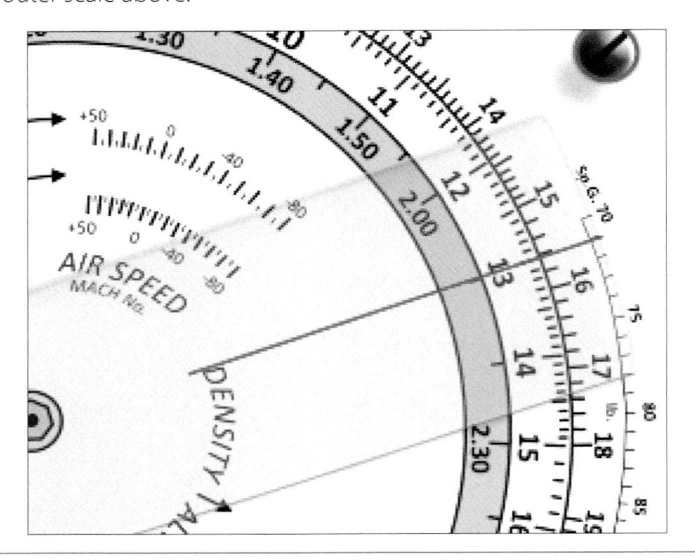

FURTHER READING: APM VOLUME 3, SECTION 2, CHAPTER 8 – AIRSPEED

16. (ANSWER: A) Magnetic Heading 037°; Duration 32 minutes.

Pressure Altitude (FT)/ OAT(°C)	CAS (kt)	TAS (kt)	W/V	TR (T)	HDG (T)	Var.	HDG (M)	GS	DIST (NM)	Time
5000/+10	98	**107**	310/20	045	**034**	3W	**037**	**106**	56	**32**

The first step is to find the TAS. Using your CRP flight computer, in the AIRSPEED window, align the OAT (+10° C) with the pressure altitude (5000 ft); find the CAS (98 kt) on the inner rotating scale and read off the TAS above it on the outer scale above.

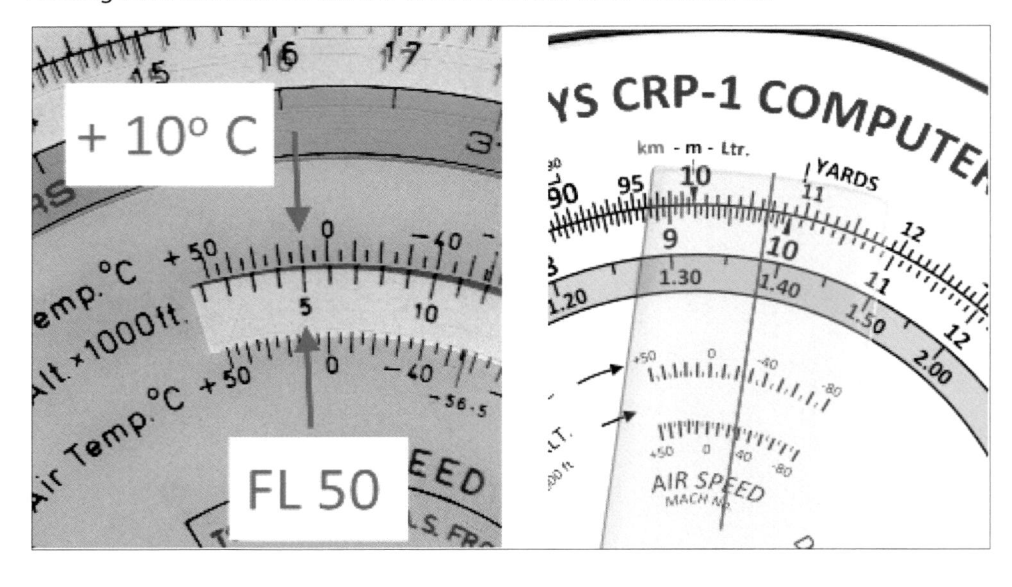

Next, find the magnetic heading:

1. Set the wind direction (310) on the rotating inner scale under the Index on the fixed outer scale.
2. Set the centre circle on a convenient speed arc – 100 is a handy round number. Mark down the wind speed, 20 knots for this question.
3. Move the sliding scale so that the centre circle is over the TAS 107.
4. Rotate the inner scale so that the measured true track, 045, is now below the index. Note the wind mark is now displaced 11° to the right.
5. Rotate the inner scale 11° to the right, 045 is now below 11° on the right hand side of the fixed drift scale. What we are aiming for is parity, so check that the wind dot still indicates 11° right. In this case it does and no further adjustment is needed.
6. Read off the true heading under the Index = 034°.
7. Apply the variation, in this case 3° W. Remember "East is Least, West is Best", the variation is West, hence we add it giving a magnetic heading of 037°.
8. Finally, before putting the CRP away not the ground speed = 106 kt

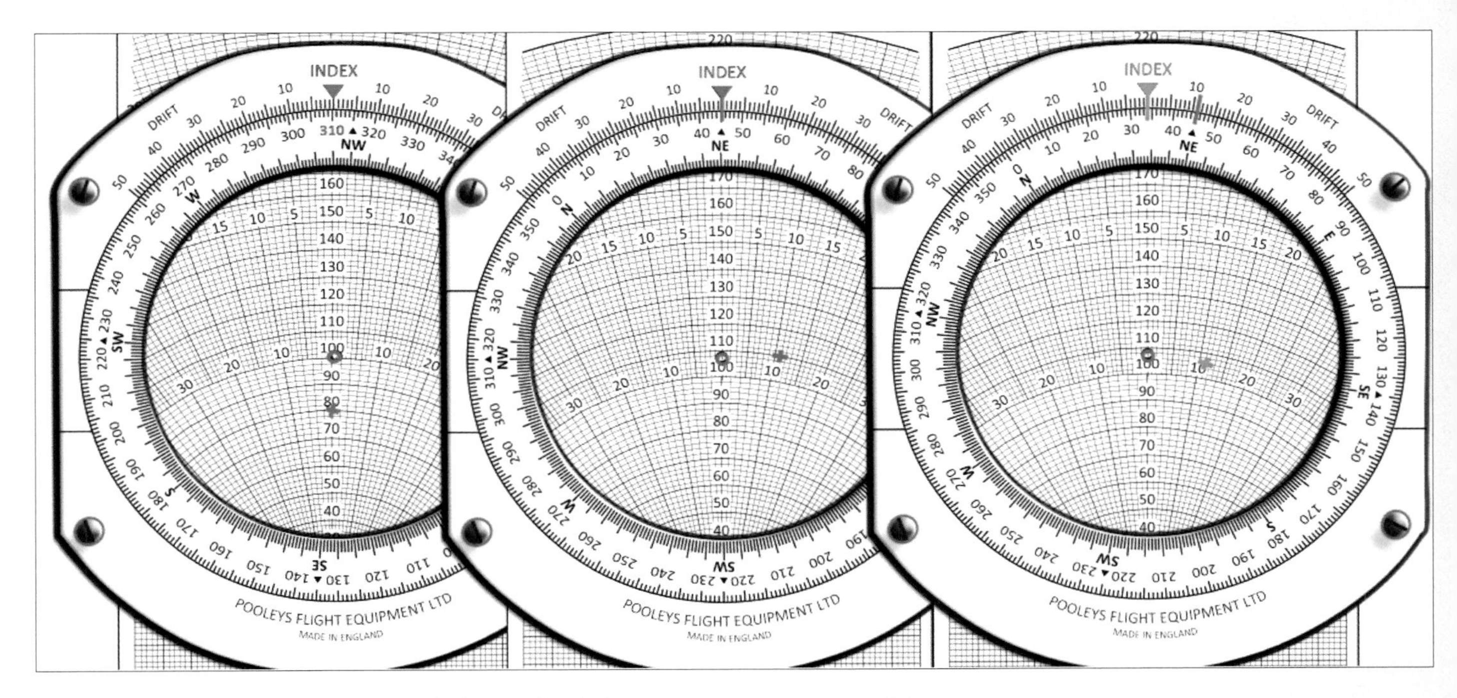

Making a small sketch is a good idea to check that your answers are sensible:

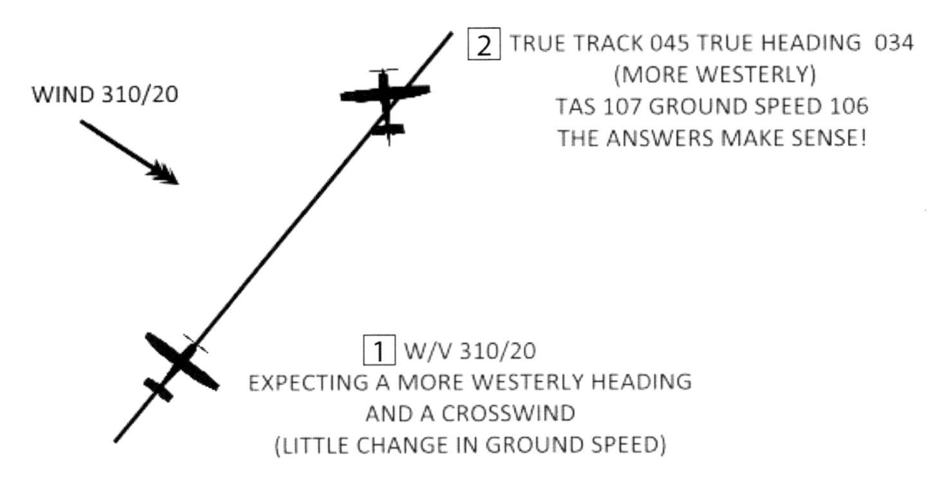

Lastly, we are asked to find the time it will take to fly the leg:

OUTER SCALE:	DISTANCE	SPEED
INNER SCALE:	TIME	60

Again, it is useful to have an idea of the answer we are expecting to get so that we can be confident that we have read the computer correctly. Very roughly a ground speed of 106 knots is close to 120, which would give us a rate over the ground of 2 nm per minute. The distance, 56 nm, divided by 2 gives an answer of 28, so we are anticipating an answer just over 30 minutes.

Back to the CRP, set the "60" mark on the rotating inner scale under the ground speed, here 106 knots. Re-set the moving lubber line to 56 nm (the distance) on the outer scale – here it helps to remember from school "speed = distance over time" i.e. distance is set on the outer scale OVER time on the inner.

Read off the time on the top of the inner scale 31.8 minutes.

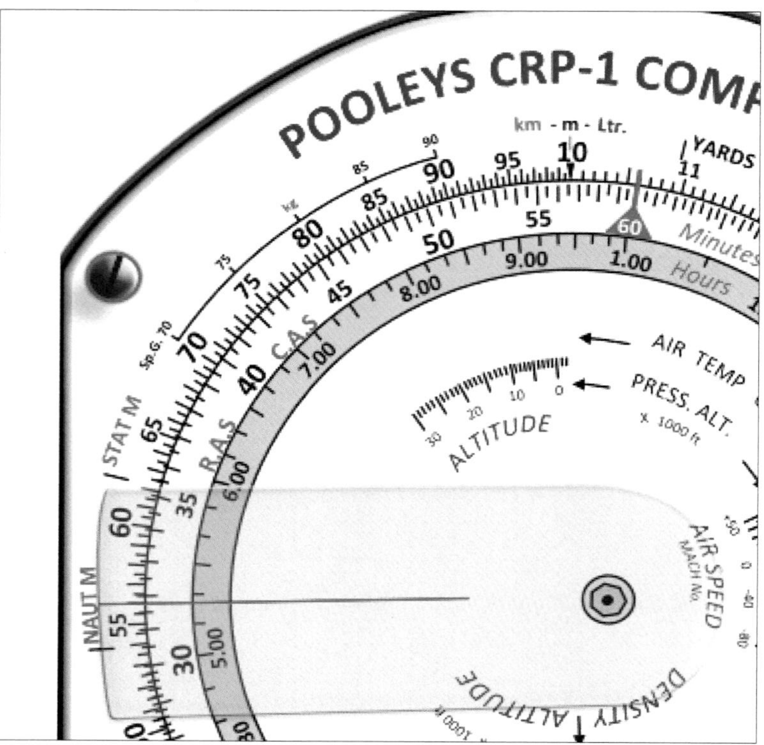

FURTHER READING: APM VOLUME 3, SECTION 2, CHAPTER 9 – DRIFT

17. **(Answer: D)** 220/30.

1. Place centre dot on TAS, 110 knots
2. Set Heading, 165, under the index
3. The difference between heading and track is 14°. It is port drift as the track is to the left of the heading

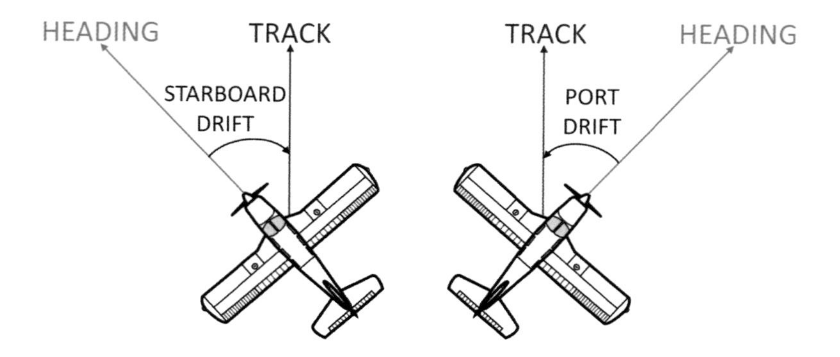

4. Follow the arc representing the groundspeed, 96 knots, and make a mark to represent the drift - 14° left
5. Now, move the centre dot down to the wind component grid.
6. Rotate the inner disc until your wind mark is below the centre dot.
7. Read off the wind direction under the index, 217 degrees and the velocity under the mark on the wind component grid, here 30 knots.

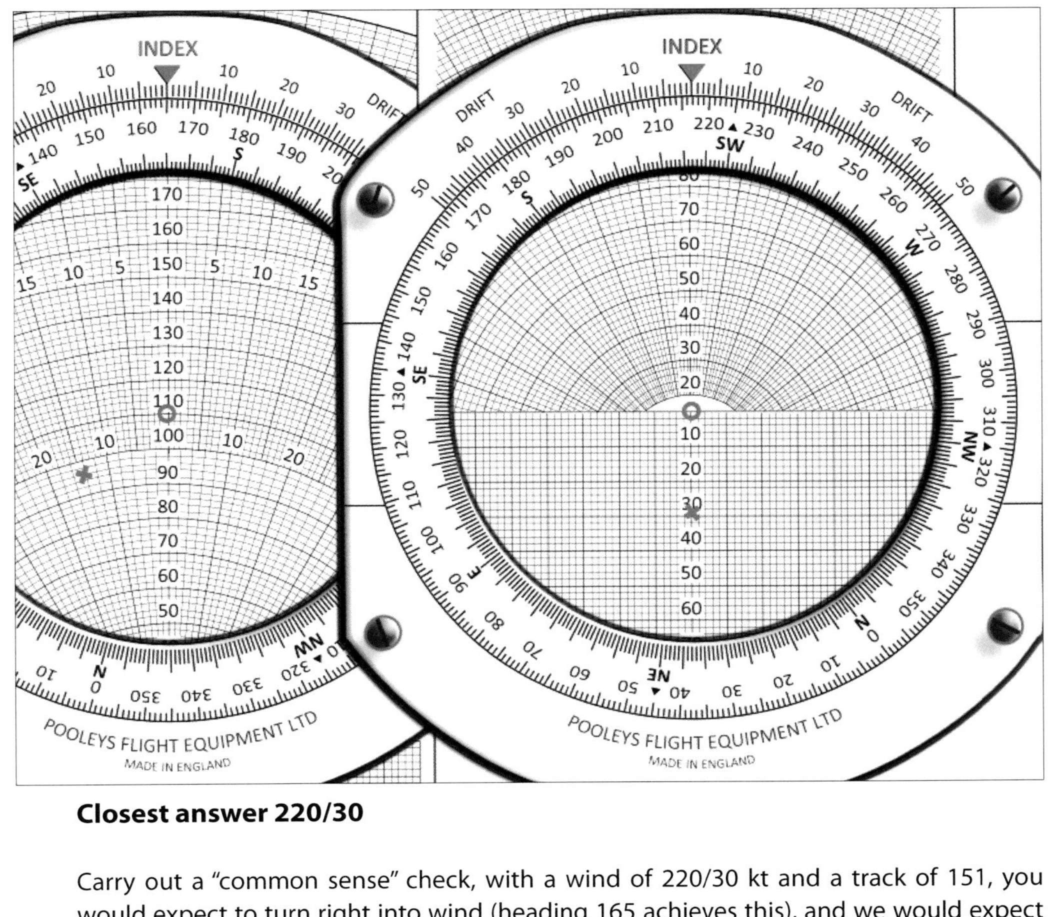

Closest answer 220/30

Carry out a "common sense" check, with a wind of 220/30 kt and a track of 151, you would expect to turn right into wind (heading 165 achieves this), and we would expect a reduction in groundspeed due to a headwind. The answer we obtained therefore seems sensible.

FURTHER READING: APM VOLUME 3, SECTION 2, CHAPTER 9 – DRIFT

18. (Answer: C) 1119 UTC.

To begin find the ground speed:

1. Set the wind direction (310) on the rotating inner scale under the Index on the fixed outer scale.
2. Set the centre circle on a convenient speed arc – 100 is a handy round number. Mark down the wind speed, 15 knots for this question.
3. Move the sliding scale so that the centre circle is over the TAS 102.
4. Rotate the inner scale so that the measured true track, 260, is now below the index.
5. Read off the ground speed: 92 kt

Carry out a common sense check: The difference between the heading 260 and the wind direction 310 is 50°, and we can see from the CRP that it is a headwind and can anticipate a groundspeed lower than the TAS.

Rule of Thumb:

The cross wind component can be roughly calculated using the sine of number of degrees between the heading (or runway direction) and the wind direction. Similarly the cosine of that angle can be used to find a head or tailwind component.

SINE	CROSSWIND COMPONENT
30° = 0.5	50% of wind speed
40° = 0.6	60% of wind speed
50° = 0.7	70% of wind speed
60° = 0.9	90% of wind speed

COSINE	HEAD/TAIL WIND COMPONENT
30° = 0.9	90% of wind speed
40° = 0.75	75% of wind speed
50° = 0.6	60% of wind speed
60° = 0.5	50% of wind speed

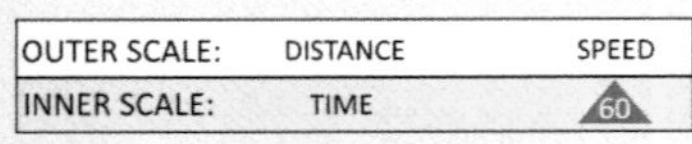

15 x 0.6 = 9 knots
102 – 9 = 93 knots ground speed

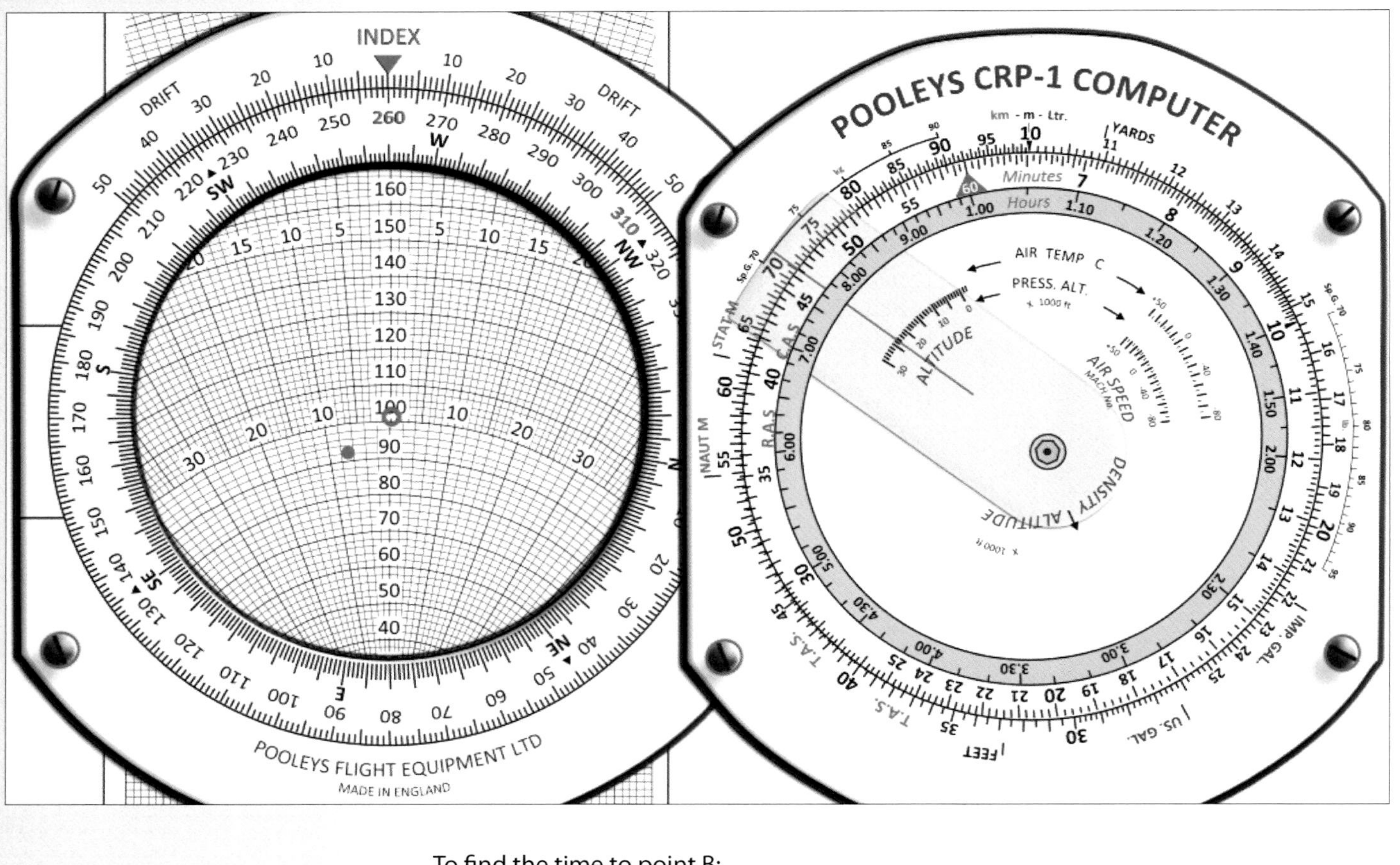

To find the time to point B:

1. Place the ground speed, 92 kt, over the time index
2. On the outer scale find the distance 71 nm
3. Read off the time on the inner scale: 46.5 minutes
4. Again a common sense check shows that if we are travelling at nearly 1.5 nm per minute (900 kts): 71 ÷ 1.5 = 47 minutes

Finally, add your result to the time to find the ETA: 1030 + 46.5 = 1116.5 UTC

Closest answer 1117 UTC.

FURTHER READING: APM VOLUME 3, SECTION 2, CHAPTER 9 – DRIFT

---

19. **(Answer: C)** 91 kt. As there is no head or tail wind component the groundspeed is the TAS.

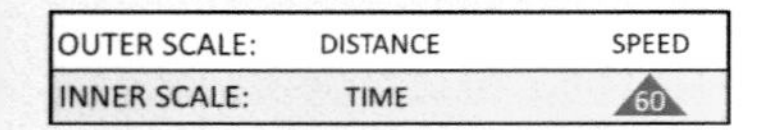

To find the TAS:

1. Set time, 50 minutes, below distance 80 nm.
2. Above the index, read off the speed: 96 kt

Stage two is to convert TAS to CAS:

3. In the airspeed window, set temperature, –10° C against the pressure altitude of FL 50.
4. Below TAS, 96 kt, on the outer scale, read off the CAS on the inner scale: 91 kt

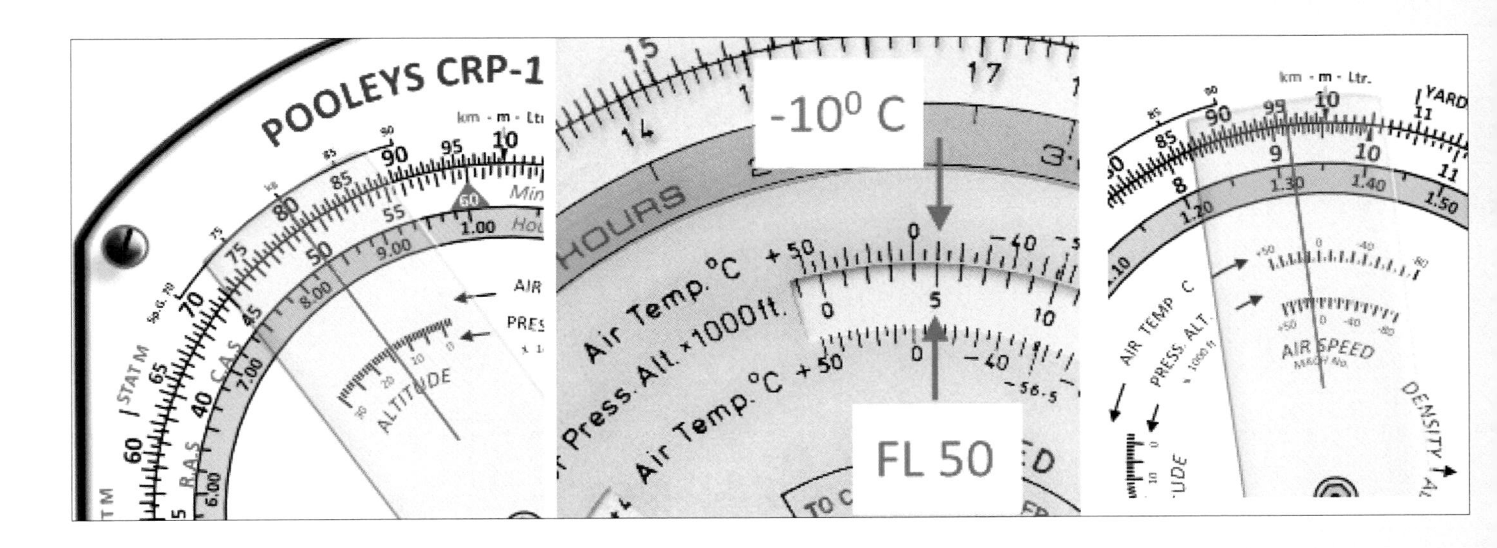

FURTHER READING: APM VOLUME 3, SECTION 2, CHAPTER 10 – TIMING AND FUEL MANAGEMENT

END OF EXPLANATIONS PAPER 1

INTENTIONALLY BLANK

NAVIGATION PAPER 2

1. The correct Q code for a true bearing from a VDF station is:

- **a.** QDM
- **b.** QDR
- **c.** QUJ
- **d.** QTE

2. A Class B VDF bearing is accurate to:

- **a.** ± 5°
- **b.** ± 2°
- **c.** ± 10°
- **d.** ± 8°

3. The accuracy of a VDF may be decreased by:

- **a.** Night effect
- **b.** Thunderstorms
- **c.** Coastal effect
- **d.** Site and propagation errors

4. How may the range of primary radar be increased?

- **a.** By increasing the rate of rotation of the radar head
- **b.** By increasing the width of the radar head antenna which will produce a long and narrow beam
- **c.** By locating the radar head at an elevation above surrounding obstacles
- **d.** By reducing the width of the radar head antenna which will produce a long and narrow beam

5. With regard to the illustration below, which of the following statements is correct?

- **a.** "A" is a primary radar return
- **b.** "B" is a primary and secondary radar return
- **c.** "C" is a primary and secondary radar return with Altitude information
- **d.** "B" is a primary return, secondary information is provided on a separate screen

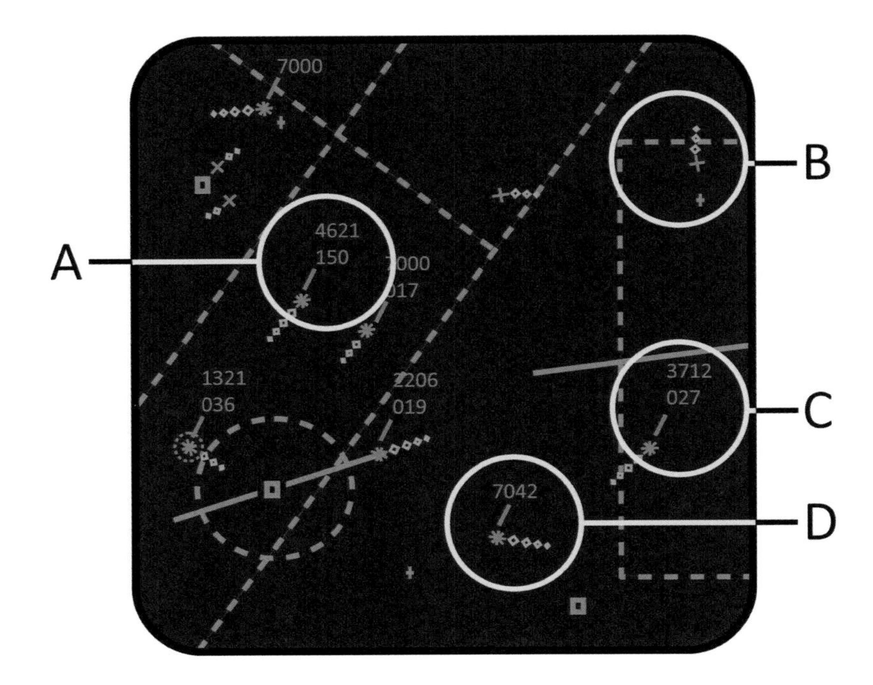

6. A rhumb line may be defined as:

a. A line on the Earth which represents the shortest distance between any two places
b. A line joining places of equal magnetic variation
c. Any line drawn on a chart using a Lambert projection
d. A line on the Earth which crosses all meridians at the same angle

7. Sunrise is when:

a. The upper limb of the Sun appears to touch the horizon
b. The lower limb of the Sun appears to touch the horizon
c. The upper limb of the Sun is 6° below the horizon
d. The upper limb of the Sun is 6° above the horizon

8. You are flying and maintaining a true track of 255° T with 7° right drift. The magnetic variation in the area is 6° E, and from the compass card you know that the deviation is 2° W. What is the aircraft's compass heading?

a. 248° C
b. 248° T
c. 252° C
d. 244° C

9. If an aircraft flies due north along a meridian from latitude 28° 30′ S to 15° N, in nautical miles what distance is covered?

a. 2,580 nm
b. 810 nm
c. 2,610 nm
d. 2,550 nm

10. A magnetic compass is most accurate

a. At low latitudes
b. At either 33° North or South
c. At high latitudes
d. At mid latitudes, around 45° North or South

11. The equipment associated with Secondary Surveillance Radar (SSR) are:

a. A transponder on the ground and DME in the air
b. A transponder in the air and PPI on the ground
c. A transponder in the air and DME on the ground
d. A transponder on the ground and SPI on the ground

12. An aircraft is flying between two points 80 nm apart, after 20 nm the aircraft is found to be 3 nm to the right of track. In order to route directly to the destination what heading correction is necessary?

a. 14° right
b. 3° right
c. 9° left
d. 12° left

13. Which radio navigation system operates using the principle of phase comparison?

a. DME
b. GPS
c. VOR
d. VDF

14. Overhead point A the fuel contents are 17 USG. 19 minutes later, over point B, the fuel contents is 15 USG. Your destination, C, is 42 minutes away.

Assuming the fuel flow remains constant and a Specific Gravity (Sp. G) of 0.72, how much fuel will remain, in lb, when overhead C?

- **a.** 27 lb
- **b.** 62.5 lb
- **c.** 10.5 lb
- **d.** 75 lb

15. An aircraft is flying at an indicated air speed (IAS) of 110 knots at FL 40. The OAT is -5° C, what is the aircraft's true airspeed (TAS)? Ignore position and instrument errors.

- **a.** 117 kt
- **b.** 114 kt
- **c.** 240 kt
- **d.** 109 kt

16. Complete the table below. From the completed table what is the magnetic heading and duration for the leg?

Pressure Altitude (FT)/ OAT(°C)	CAS (kt)	TAS (kt)	W/V	TR (T)	HDG (T)	Var.	HDG (M)	GS	DIST (NM)	Time
7000/+15	120		160/25	300		3W			83	

- **a.** Magnetic Heading 291°; Duration 32 minutes
- **b.** Magnetic Heading 296°; Duration 42 minutes
- **c.** Magnetic Heading 296°; Duration 32 minutes
- **d.** Magnetic Heading 291°; Duration 42 minutes

17. Given the following details calculate the wind velocity:

TAS	130 knots
GROUNDSPEED	141 knots
TRUE HEADING	116 degrees
TRUE TRACK	120 degrees

- **a.** 360/20
- **b.** 340/15
- **c.** 290/15
- **d.** 310/25

18. Your aircraft is maintaining a TAS of 94 knots and arrives overhead turning point A at 1450 UTC. Turning point B is 102 nm away using a track of 010° T. Calculate your ETA at B using a forecast wind of 220/25 kt.

- **a.** 1612 UTC
- **b.** 1552 UTC
- **c.** 1602 UTC
- **d.** 1542 UTC

19. Your destination is 77 nm away, you must arrive in not less than 42 minutes. If you are flying at FL 50 and the OAT is + 10° C? what is the minimum Calibrated Airspeed CAS required to arrive at the desired time? Assume no head or tail wind component.

- **a.** 91 kt
- **b.** 111 kt
- **c.** 101 kt
- **d.** 97 kt

END OF NAVIGATION PAPER 2

INTENTIONALLY BLANK

NAVIGATION PAPER 2: ANSWERS

No	A	B	C	D
1				X
2	X			
3				X
4			X	
5			X	
6				X
7	X			
8				X
9			X	
10	X			
11		X		
12				X
13			X	
14		X		
15		X		
16			X	
17		X		
18				X
19			X	

CORRECT ANSWERS: PERCENTAGES					
15	16	17	18	19	20
75%	80%	85%	90%	95%	100%

NAVIGATION PAPER 2: EXPLANATIONS

1. **(Answer: D)** QTE is the true bearing of the aircraft from the station.

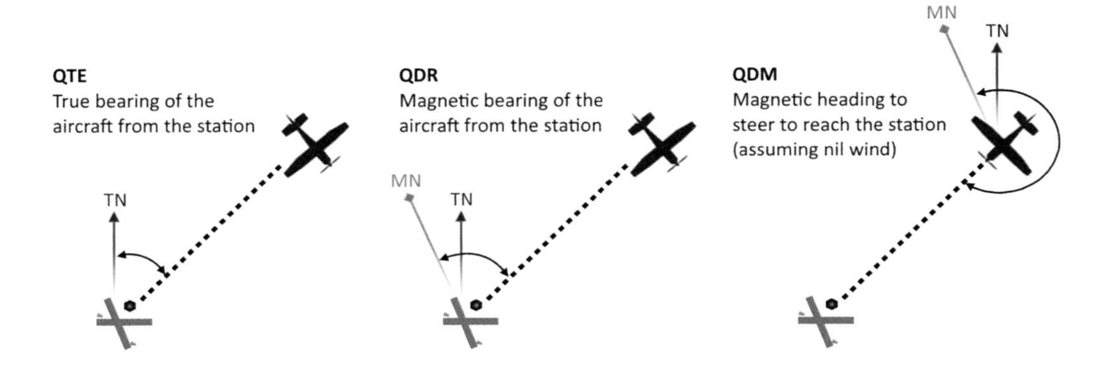

FURTHER READING: APM VOLUME 3, SECTION 4, CHAPTER 22 – THE NDB AND THE ADF

2. **(Answer: A)**

Accuracy of VDF Bearings
Class A +/- 2 degrees
Class B +/- 5 degrees
Class C +/- 10 degrees
Class D accuracy less than class C

FURTHER READING: APM VOLUME 3, SECTION 4, CHAPTER 23 – VHF DIRECTION FINDING (VDF)

3. **(Answer: D)** VDF operates in the VHF band and therefore its accuracy can be decreased by:

a. Site errors: caused by reflections from buildings, uneven ground etc.
b. Propagation errors: caused by the radio wave scalloping over differing terrain, these are particularly noticeable at long range from the VDF station

FURTHER READING: APM VOLUME 3, SECTION 4, CHAPTER 23 – VHF DIRECTION FINDING (VDF)

4. **(Answer: C)** Primary radar uses UHF (ultra- high frequency) transmissions which are line of sight; buildings, high ground and the curvature of the earth can cause radar shadows, meaning that objects in these areas are not detected. One way to try to lessen these effects is to site the radar antenna on high ground above surrounding obstacles.

An approximate range can be calculated using one of the following formulae:
Radar range = √1.5 x height above ground level in ft (nm)
Or
Radar range = 1.22 √ height above ground level in ft (nm)

FURTHER READING: APM VOLUME 3, SECTION 4, CHAPTER 18 – RADAR

5. (Answer: C)

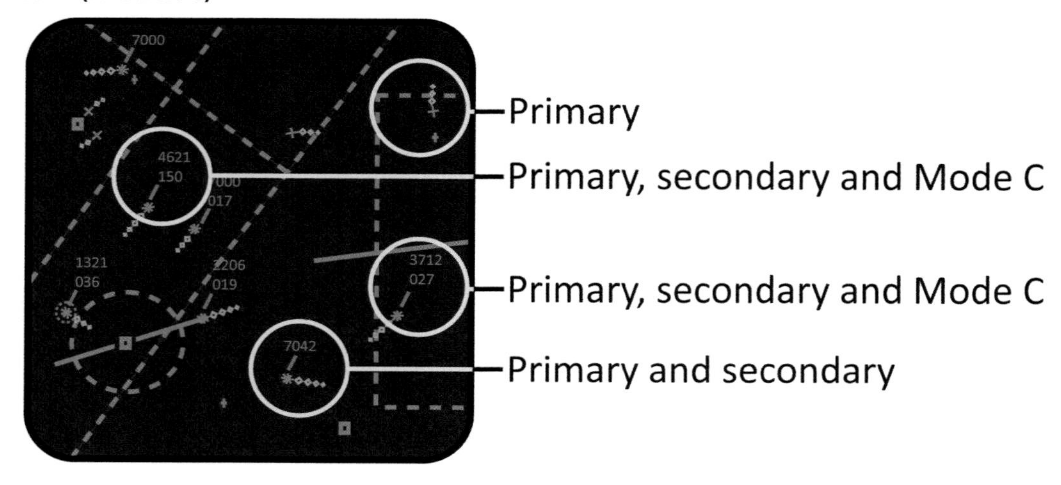

FURTHER READING: APM VOLUME 3, SECTION 4, CHAPTER 18 – RADAR

6. (Answer: D) A rhumb line is a line which crosses all meridians of longitude at the same angle.

- A straight line drawn on a Transverse Mercator projection is a rhumb line.
- All parallels of latitude are rhumb lines, since they intersect with the meridians at the same angle.
- As a constant angle is maintained a rhumb line is easier to fly.

FURTHER READING: APM VOLUME 3, SECTION 1, CHAPTER 2 – AERONAUTICAL CHARTS

7. (Answer: A) Sunrise and sunset conventionally refer to the times when the upper limb of the disc of the Sun is on the horizon.

Civil Twilight:

In the morning: starts when the centre of the Sun's disc is 6° below the horizon and finishes at sunrise.

In the evening: starts at sunset and ends when the centre of the Sun's disc is 6° below the horizon.

FURTHER READING: APM VOLUME 3, SECTION 1, CHAPTER 3 – TIME

8. (Answer: D) The first stage is to find the aircraft's true heading. Drift is measured from the heading (nose) to the track, and is classified in degrees port or starboard of heading.

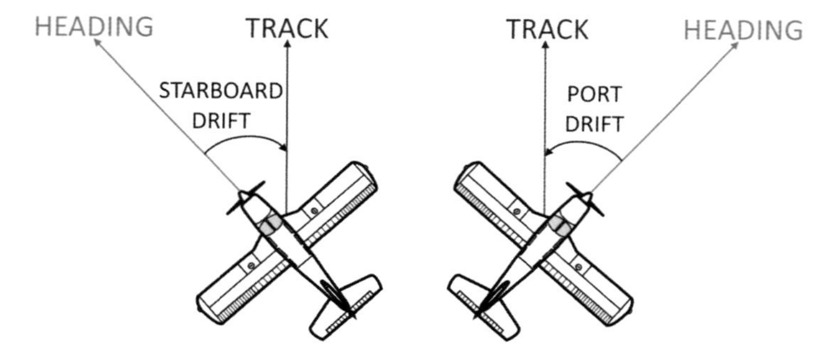

In this case the true track is 255 and the drift is to the right (starboard). Therefore, the true heading is: 255 – 7 = 248° T

The next stage is to use **T v M d C**, and to create a table containing the known details.

True Heading	Variation	Magnetic Heading	Deviation	Compass Heading
248	6E		2W	

Remember also "East is Least; West is Best" – meaning that easterly corrections are subtracted and westerly ones added **when working from left to right**. It is now possible to complete the table.

True Heading	Variation	Magnetic Heading	Deviation	Compass Heading
248	6E	**242**	2W	**244**

The compass heading is therefore 244° C.

FURTHER READING: APM VOLUME 3, SECTION 1, CHAPTER 4– THE MAGNETIC COMPASS AND DIRECTION

9. **(Answer: C)** A nautical mile is defined as a unit of distance equal to one minute (')of arc on the earth's surface. Each degree of latitude is made up of 60 minutes and therefore equates to 60 nm. As long as the movement is along a great circle, i.e. any meridian or the equator, the conversion between change in latitude and distance is straight forward.

To begin with find the total distance travelled in degrees and minutes. In this case the locations given are in opposite hemispheres and so the latitudes are added together: 28° 30′+ 15 = 43° 30′

To find the distance in nm multiply each full degree travelled by 60: 43 x 60 = 2,580 nm
And add any extra minutes: 2,580 + (30 minutes at 1 nm per minute) = 2,610 nm.

FURTHER READING: APM VOLUME 3, SECTION 2, CHAPTER 9 – DRIFT

10. **(Answer: A)** A magnetic compass is most accurate at low latitudes.

The compass suffers from both turning and acceleration errors as a result of magnetic dip, or "z", leading to the weight of the magnet not being directly underneath the pivot. Magnetic dip is due to the magnet trying to align itself with the earth's magnetic field which is practically horizontal at the equator, but almost vertical at the poles. Where dip is minimal the compass will be at its most accurate and this will occur at low latitudes. Arranging the magnet as a pendulum does alleviate some of the problem, but will not eradicate it totally.

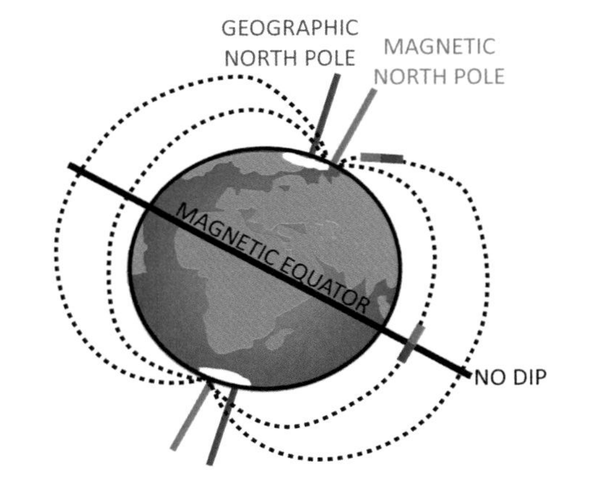

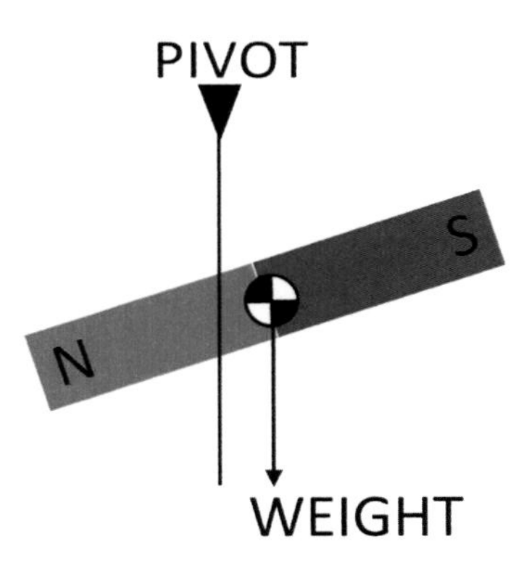

FURTHER READING: APM VOLUME 3, SECTION 1, CHAPTER 4– THE MAGNETIC COMPASS AND DIRECTION

11. (Answer: B) PPI stands for Plan Position Indicator and is another term for the radar screen used by controllers. It is on the PPI that the SSR information from the aircraft's transponder are displayed.

SSR

TRANSPONDER IN THE AIRCRAFT

PLAN POSITION INDICATOR DISPLAYS INFORMATION TO THE CONTROLLER ON THE GROUND

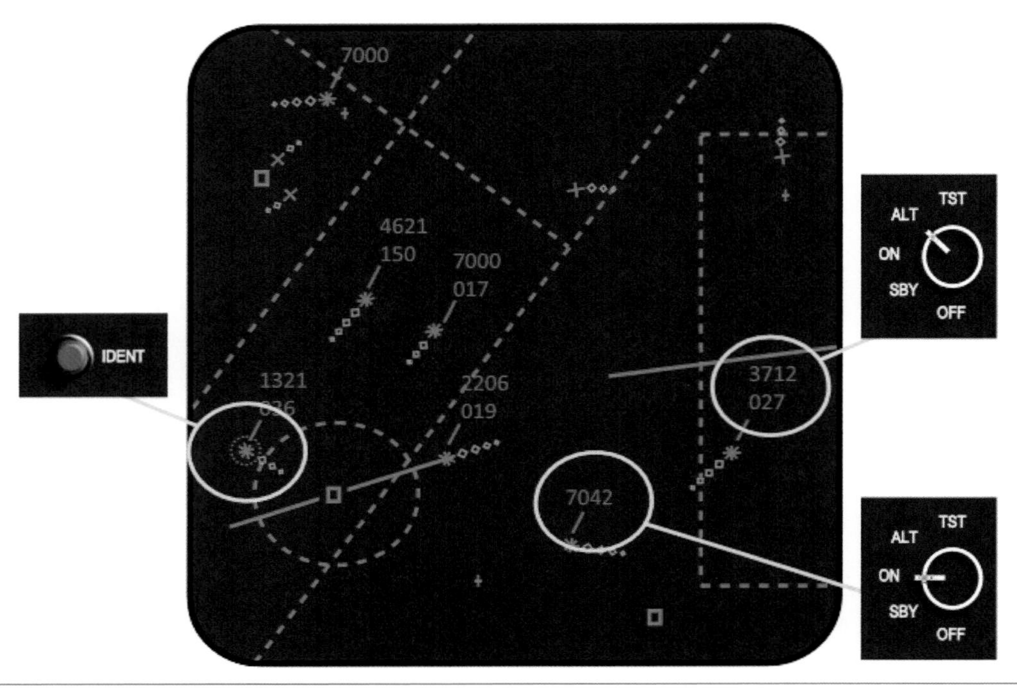

FURTHER READING: APM VOLUME 3, SECTION 4, CHAPTER 18 – RADAR

12. (Answer: A) 0817 UTC. Co-ordinated Universal Time (UTC) is the primary time standard by which the world regulates clocks and time, it is the standard used throughout aviation. UTC is also known as Zulu and is the same as GMT.

Local Mean Time (LMT) is a form of solar time and is based on the passage of the Sun over a particular location. If the longitude of a place is known LMT at that position can be calculated using the following relations:
Each degree (°) of longitude = 4 minutes difference from UTC
15 minutes (') of arc = 1 minute of time

If the longitude is WEST LMT is earlier than UTC.
If the longitude is EAST LMT is later than UTC.
We could adapt the navigation aide memoire to:
"Longitude west UTC best; longitude east UTC least".

First take the whole degrees, in this case 100 and multiply by 4:
100 x 4 = 400 minutes
Then include any additional minutes. Here, we have 45' equating to 3 minutes of time.
The total time difference is therefore 400 + 3 = 403 minutes
403 minutes = 6 hours and 43 minutes.

As Bangkok has an easterly longitude, therefore UTC is less than LMT. Subtracting 6 hours and 43 minutes from 1500 gives an answer of **0817 UTC.**

FURTHER READING: APM VOLUME 3, SECTION 1, CHAPTER 3 – TIME

13. **(Answer: D)** 12° left. Off track errors can be calculated using the "One in Sixty" Rule.

TO FIND TRACK ERROR USING CRP

OUTER SCALE:	DISTANCE OFF TRACK (nm)	TRACK ERROR (degrees)
INNER SCALE:	DISTANCE TRAVELLED (nm)	60

TO FIND CLOSING ANGLE USING CRP

OUTER SCALE:	DISTANCE OFF TRACK (nm)	CLOSING ANGLE (degrees)
INNER SCALE:	DISTANCE TO GO (nm)	60

Total heading correction to reach destination = Track error + Closing Angle
= 9° + 3° = 12°

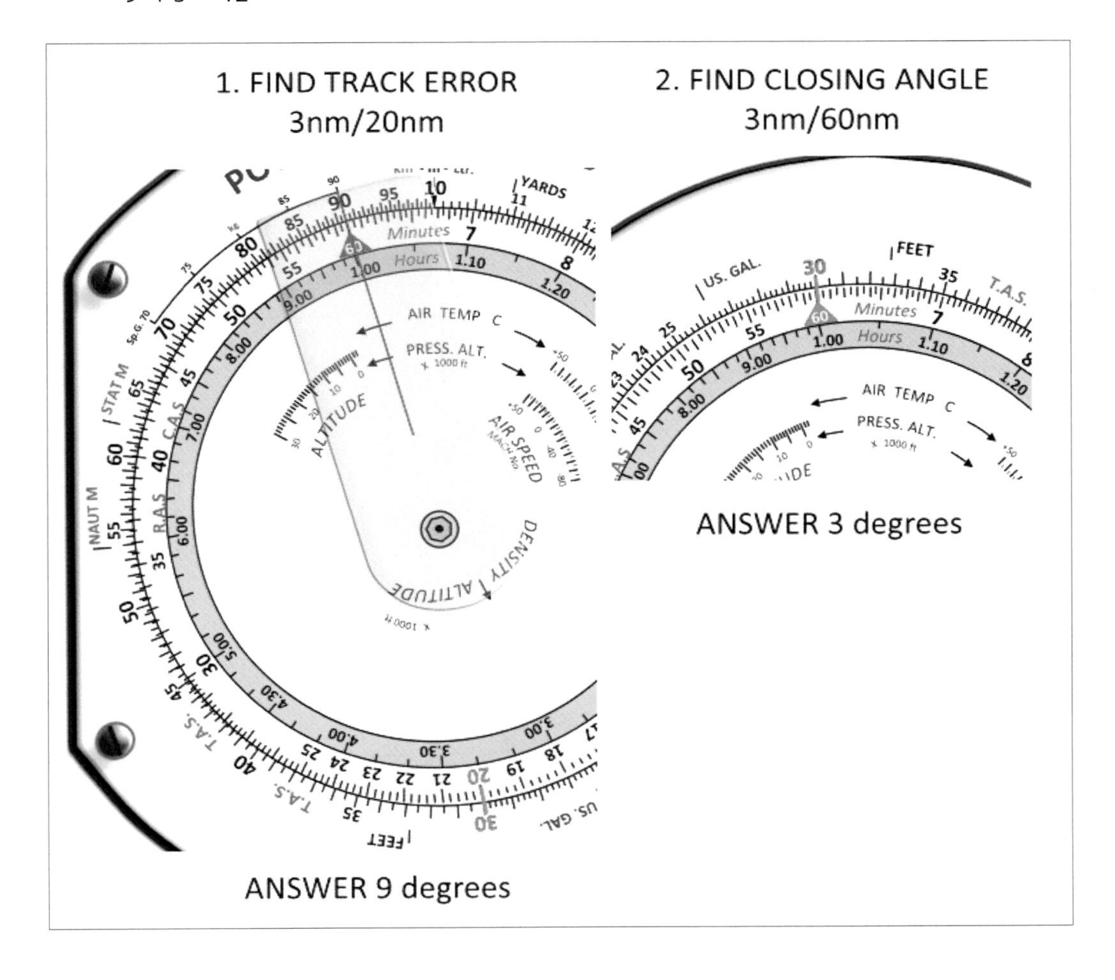

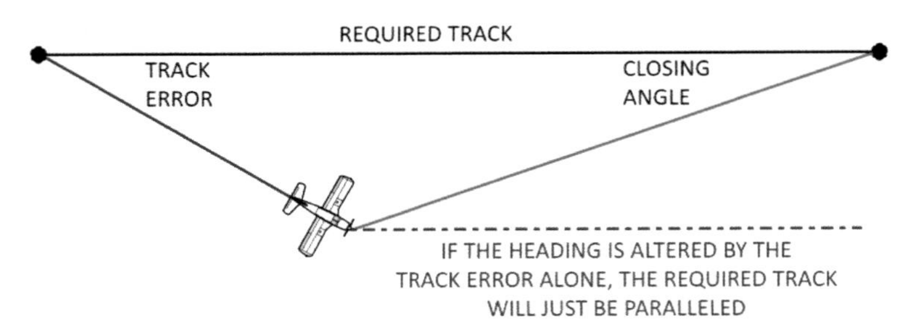

The heading must be corrected 12° left.

FURTHER READING: APM VOLUME 3, SECTION 3, CHAPTER 12 – ENROUTE NAVIGATION TECHNIQUES

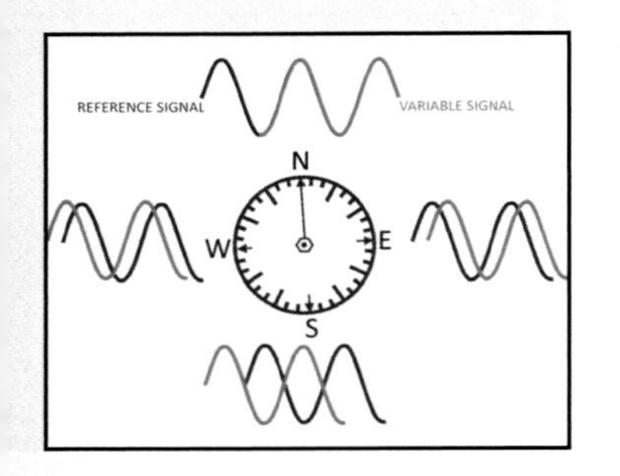

14. ANSWER C
Reference Signal (blue)
and Variable Signal (red)

14. (Answer: C) The VOR operates on the principle of phase comparison. The ground station transmits two VHF radio signals:

1. A reference signal: which is the same in all directions; and
2. A variable signal: the phase of this signal is made to vary at a constant rate throughout 360°.

The phase difference – the difference between the peaks of the radio waves - experienced by the receiver varies according to the aircraft's position around the station. When the aircraft is due north of the station the signals are in phase, i.e. they peak and trough at the same time.

The signals are then out of phase as follows:
090°M the signals are 90° out of phase
180°M the signals are 180° out of phase (anti-phase)
270°M the signals are 270° out of phase

FURTHER READING: APM VOLUME 3, SECTION 4, CHAPTER 20 – THE VOR

15. (Answer: B) 62.5 lb.

OUTER SCALE:	FUEL CONSUMPTION	FUEL
INNER SCALE:	60	TIME

Using the CRP-1 to find fuel consumption:
1. Set time elapsed between A and B, 19 minutes under the fuel used (17 – 15 = 2 USG)
2. Read fuel consumption above the time index

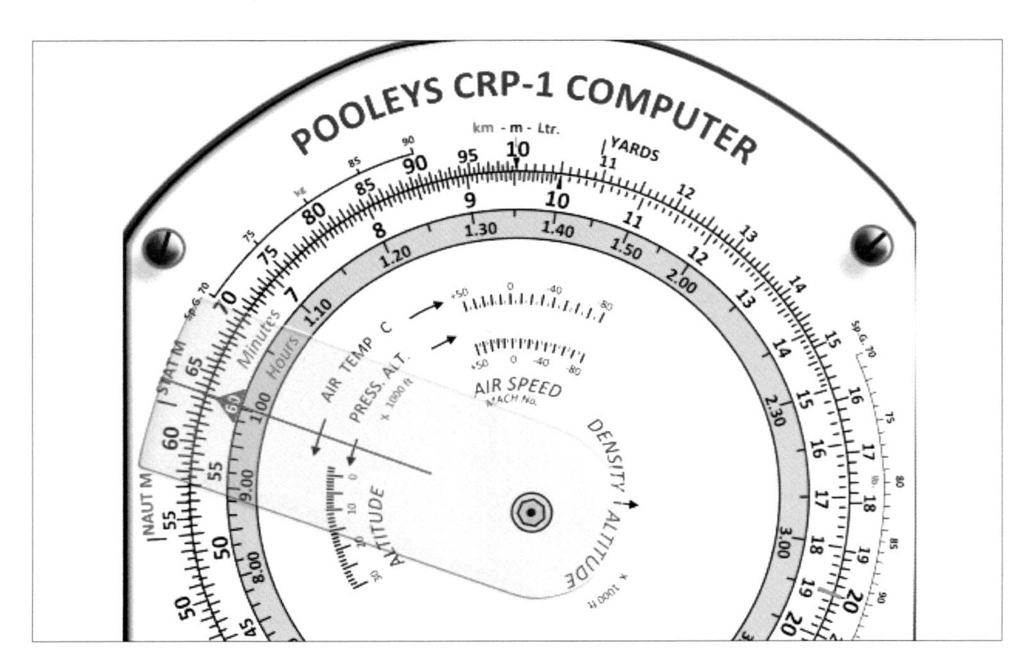

Fuel flow 6.4 USG/hr

Fuel required to reach C:

3. Keep the CRP as it is, i.e. with your calculated fuel consumption above the index
4. The next leg will take 42 minutes, find 42 on the inner rotating scale and read off the fuel required above on the outer scale.

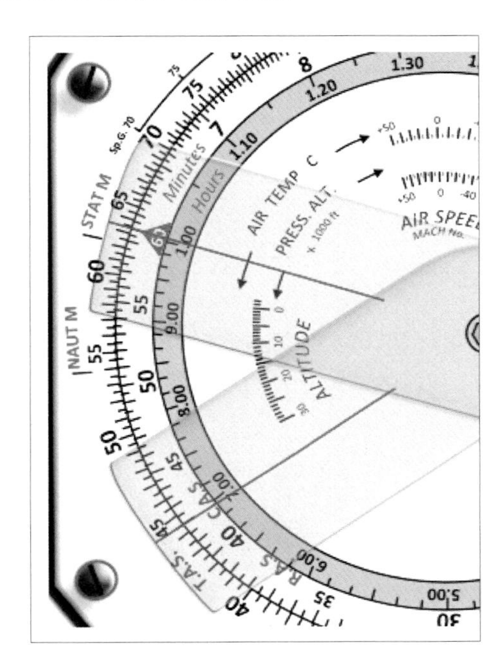

Fuel required: 4.5 USG. This answer is sensible, as this is roughly 70% of the hourly consumption.

Therefore overhead C the remaining fuel will be: **15 – 4.5 = 10.5 USG**

To find the weight of fuel in lb:

5. Set the amount of fuel, 10.5 USG, on the inner scale below the USG index
6. Set the guide line to the Sp.G scale for lb (be careful – there is a scale in kg as well!)
7. Read off the weight in lb in the inner scale

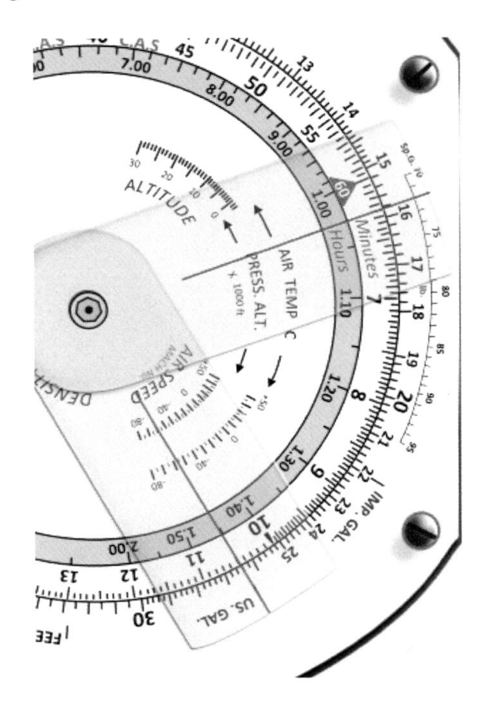

10.5 USG weighs 62.5 lb

Check: A handy figure to commit to memory, is that one USG with a Specific Gravity of 0.72 weighs 6 lb. 10.5 USG x 6 = 63 lb.

FURTHER READING: APM VOLUME 3, SECTION 2, CHAPTER 10 – TIMING AND FUEL MANAGEMENT

16. (Answer: B) 114 kt.

1. In the AIRSPEED window, align the OAT with the pressure altitude

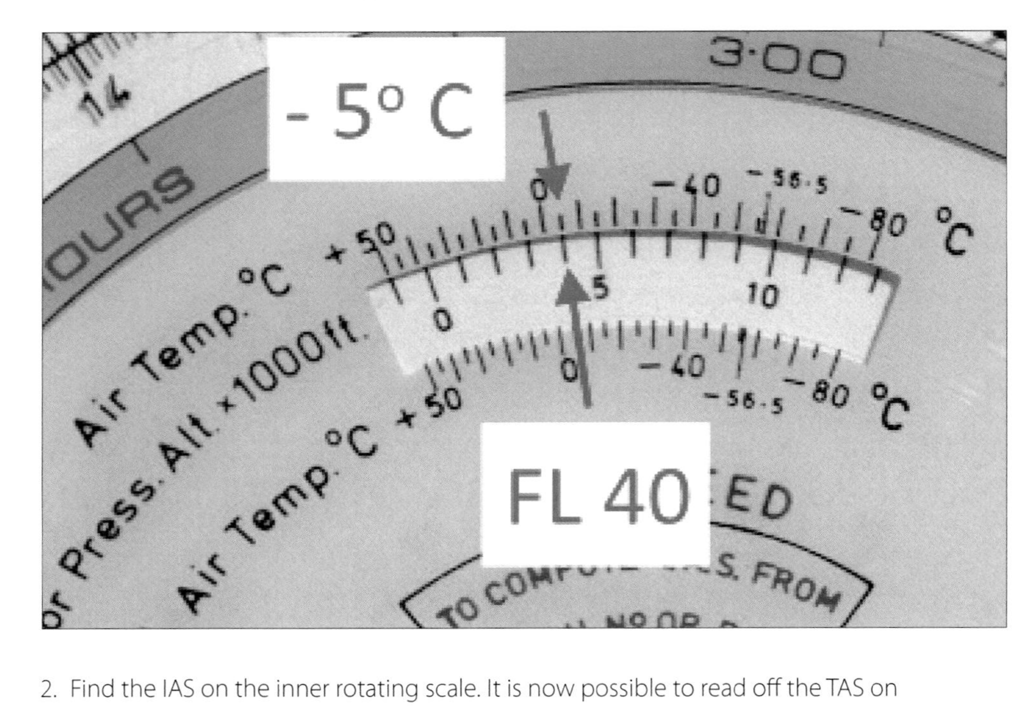

2. Find the IAS on the inner rotating scale. It is now possible to read off the TAS on the outer scale above.

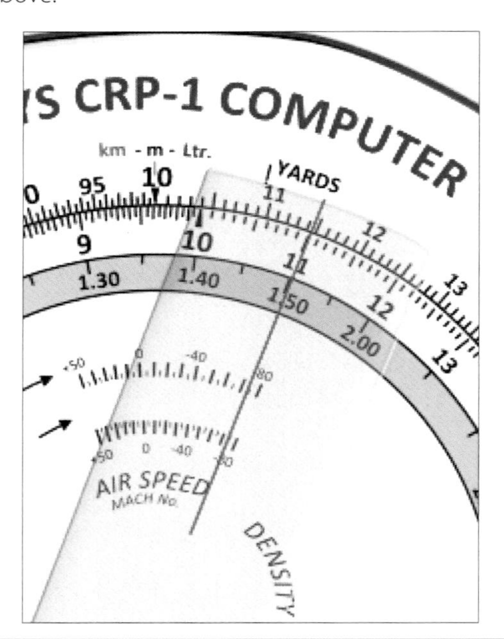

FURTHER READING: APM VOLUME 3, SECTION 2, CHAPTER 8 – AIRSPEED

17. (ANSWER: C) Magnetic Heading 296°; Duration 32 minutes.

Pressure Altitude (FT)/ OAT(°C)	CAS (kt)	TAS (kt)	W/V	TR (T)	HDG (T)	Var.	HDG (M)	GS	DIST (NM)	Time
7000/+15	120	**137**	160/25	300	**293**	3W	**296**	**156**	83	**32**

The first step is to find the TAS. Using your CRP flight computer, in the AIRSPEED window, align the OAT (+15° C) with the pressure altitude (7000 ft); find the CAS (120 kt) on the inner rotating scale and read off the TAS above it on the outer scale above.

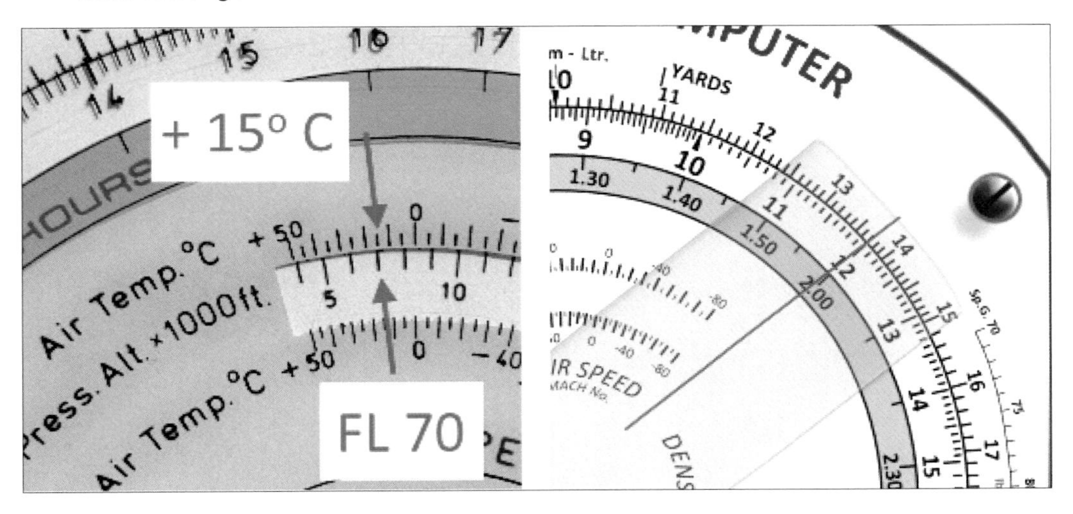

Next, find the magnetic heading:

1. Set the wind direction (160) on the rotating inner scale under the Index on the fixed outer scale.
2. Set the centre circle on a convenient speed arc – 100 is a handy round number. Mark down the wind speed, 25 knots for this question.
3. Move the sliding scale so that the centre circle is over the TAS 137.
4. Rotate the inner scale so that the measured true track, 300, is now below the index. Note the wind mark is now displaced 6° to the right.
5. Rotate the inner scale 6° to the right, 300 is now below 6° on the right hand side of the fixed drift scale. However, now the wind dot indicates 7° of starboard drift. What we are aiming for is parity, so move the rotating scale so that 300 is below 7° on the fixed drift scale and still right of the index. We have parity – the track is offset 7° and the wind mark still shows 7°.
6. Read off the true heading under the Index = 293°.
7. Apply the variation, in this case 3° W. Remember "East is Least, West is Best", the variation is West, hence we add it giving a magnetic heading of 296°.
8. Finally, before putting the CRP away note the ground speed = 156 kt

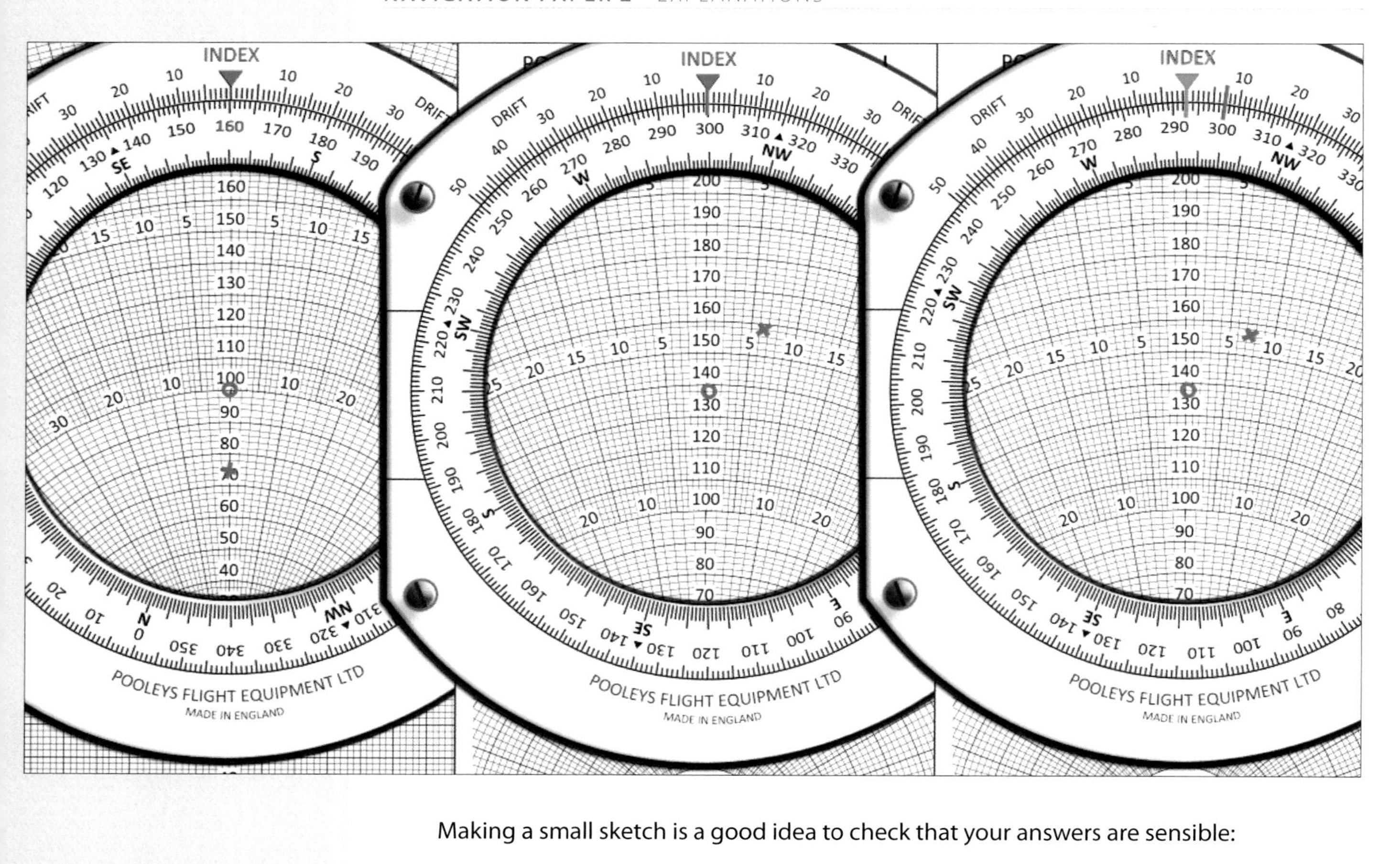

Making a small sketch is a good idea to check that your answers are sensible:

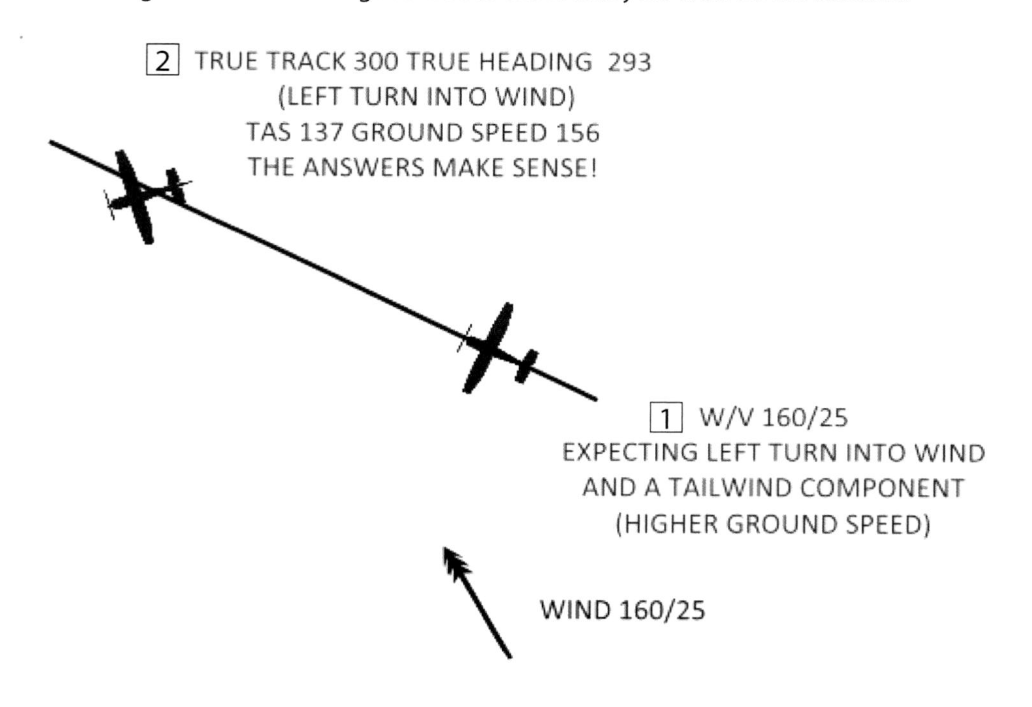

Lastly, we are asked to find the time it will take to fly the leg:

OUTER SCALE:	DISTANCE	SPEED
INNER SCALE:	TIME	60

Again, it is useful to have an idea of the answer we are expecting to get so that we can be confident that we have read the computer correctly. Very roughly a ground speed of 156 knots is close to 150, which would give us a rate over the ground of just under 2.5 nm per minute. The distance, 83 nm, divided by 2.5 gives an answer of 33.2, so we are anticipating an answer just over 30 minutes.

Back to the CRP, set the "60" mark on the rotating inner scale under the groundspeed, here 156 knots. Re-set the moving lubber line to 83 nm (the distance) on the outer scale – here it helps to remember from school "speed = distance over time" i.e. distance is set on the outer scale OVER time on the inner.

Read off the time on the top of the inner scale 32.1 minutes.

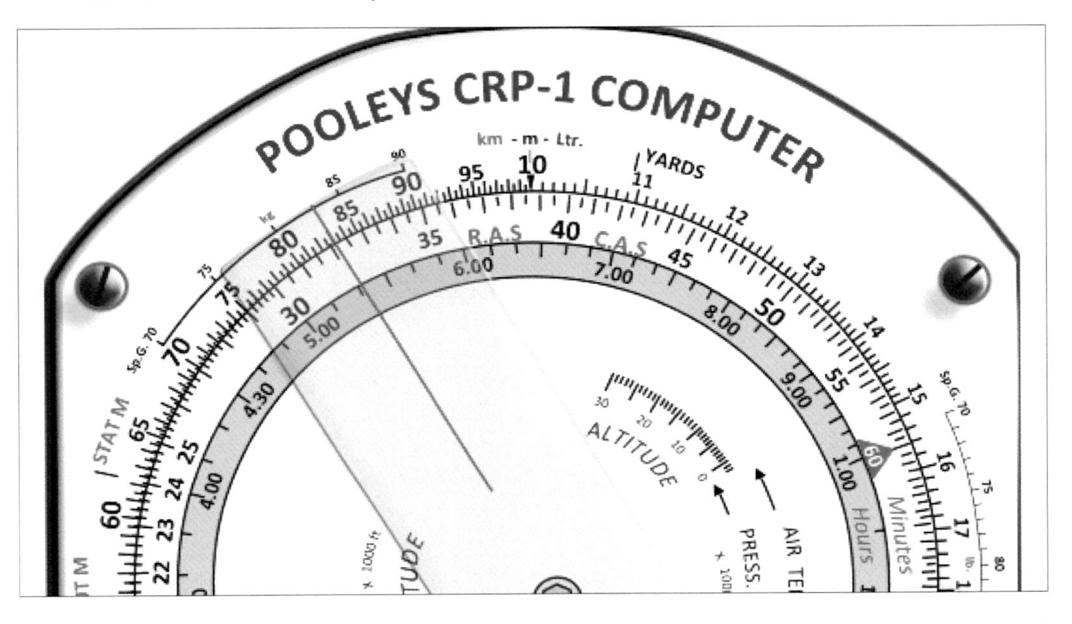

FURTHER READING: APM VOLUME 3, SECTION 2, CHAPTER 9 – DRIFT

18. (Answer: B) 340/15.

1. Place centre dot on TAS, 130 knots
2. Set Heading, 116, under the index
3. The difference between heading and track is 4°. It is starboard drift as the track is to the right of the heading

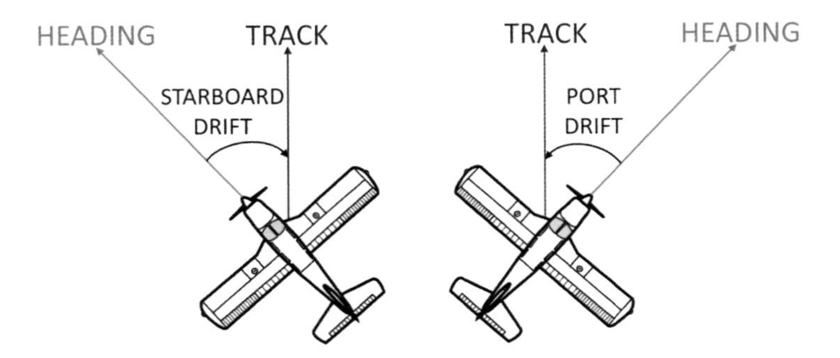

4. Follow the arc representing the groundspeed, 141 knots, and make a mark to represent the drift - 4° right
5. Now, move the centre dot down to the wind component grid.
6. Rotate the inner disc until your wind mark is below the centre dot.

7. Read off the wind direction under the index, 336 degrees and the velocity under the mark on the wind component grid, here 15 knots.

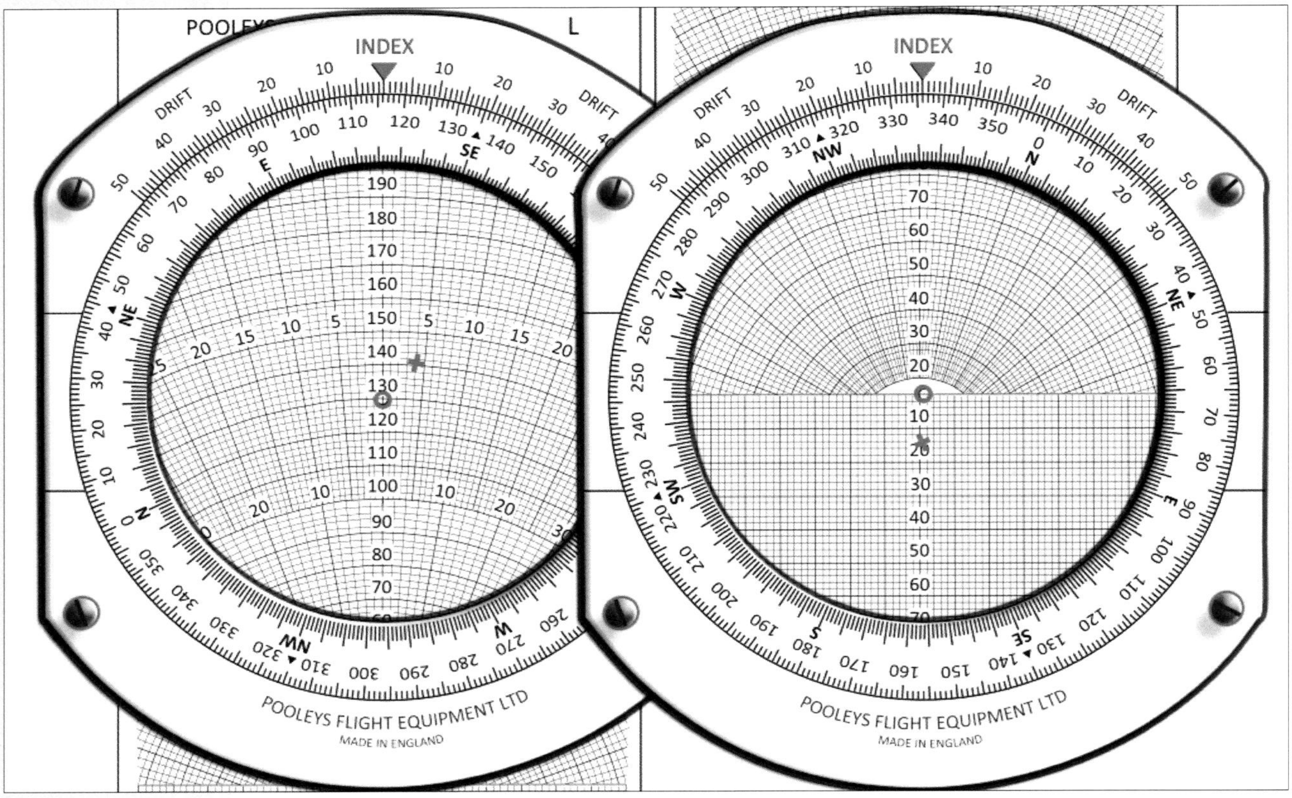

Closest answer 340/15.

Carry out a "common sense" check, with a wind of 340/15 kt and a track of 120, you would expect to turn left into wind (heading 116 achieves this), and we would expect an increase in groundspeed due to a tailwind component. The answer we obtained therefore seems sensible.

FURTHER READING: APM VOLUME 3, SECTION 2, CHAPTER 9 – DRIFT

19. (Answer: D) 1542 UTC.

To begin with find the ground speed:

1. Set the wind direction (220) on the rotating inner scale under the Index on the fixed outer scale.
2. Set the centre circle on a convenient speed arc – 100 is a handy round number. Mark down the wind speed, 25 knots for this question.
3. Move the sliding scale so that the centre circle is over the TAS 94.
4. Rotate the inner scale so that the measured true track, 010, is now below the index.
5. Read off the ground speed: 117 kt.

Carry out a common sense check: With a heading 010 and a wind direction 220 almost all of the wind speed is a tailwind; expect a big increase in ground speed. 117 kt seems reasonable.

OUTER SCALE:	DISTANCE	SPEED
INNER SCALE:	TIME	60

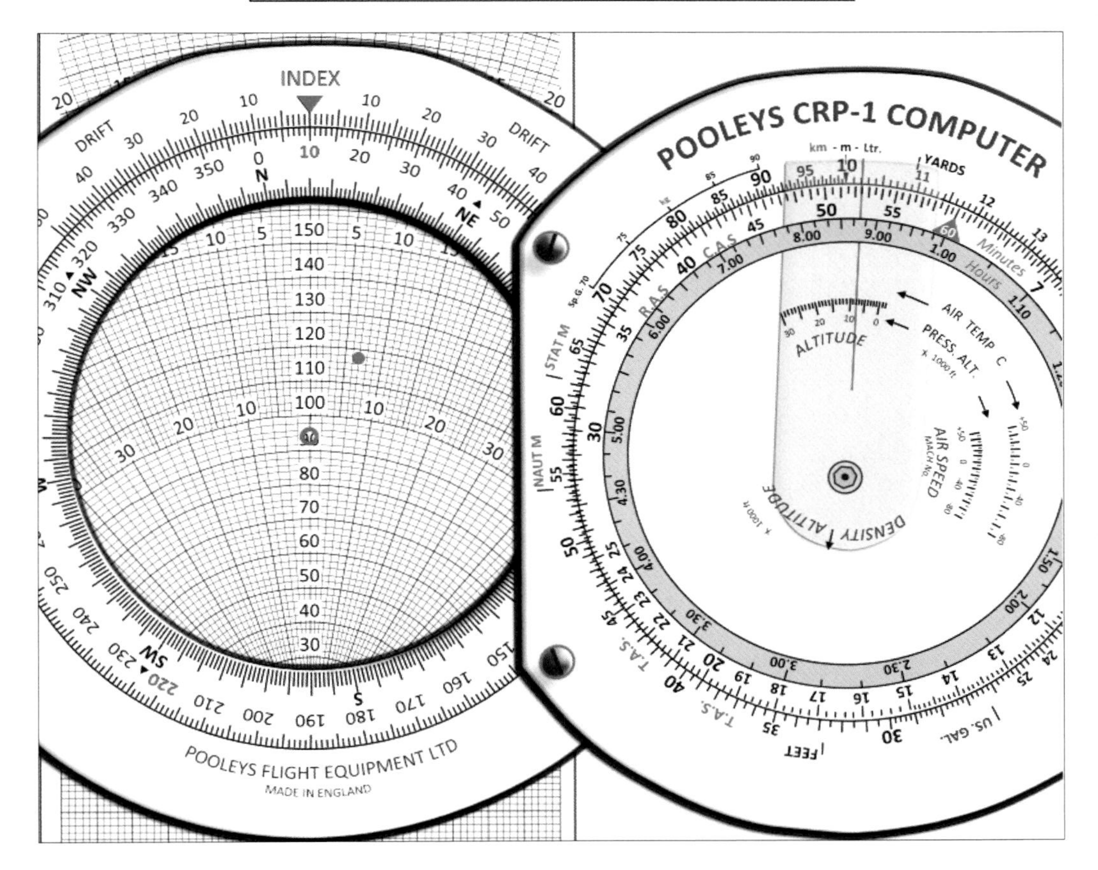

To find the time to point B:

1. Place the ground speed, 117 kt, over the time index.
2. On the outer scale find the distance 102 nm.
3. Read off the time on the inner scale: 52.5 minutes.
4. Again a common sense check shows that if we are travelling at nearly 2 nm per minute (120 kts): 102 ÷ 2 = 51 minutes.

Finally, add your result to the time to find the ETA: 1450 + 52.5 = 1542.5 UTC

Closest answer 1542 UTC.

FURTHER READING: APM VOLUME 3, SECTION 2, CHAPTER 9 – DRIFT

20. (Answer: C) 101 kt.

As there is no head or tail wind component the groundspeed is the TAS.

To find the TAS:

1. Set time, 42 minutes, below distance 77 nm.
2. Above the index, read off the speed: 110 kt.

OUTER SCALE:	DISTANCE	SPEED
INNER SCALE:	TIME	60

Stage two is to convert TAS to CAS:

3. In the airspeed window, set temperature, +10° C against the pressure altitude of FL 50.
4. Below TAS, 110 kt, on the outer scale, read off the CAS on the inner scale: 101 kt.

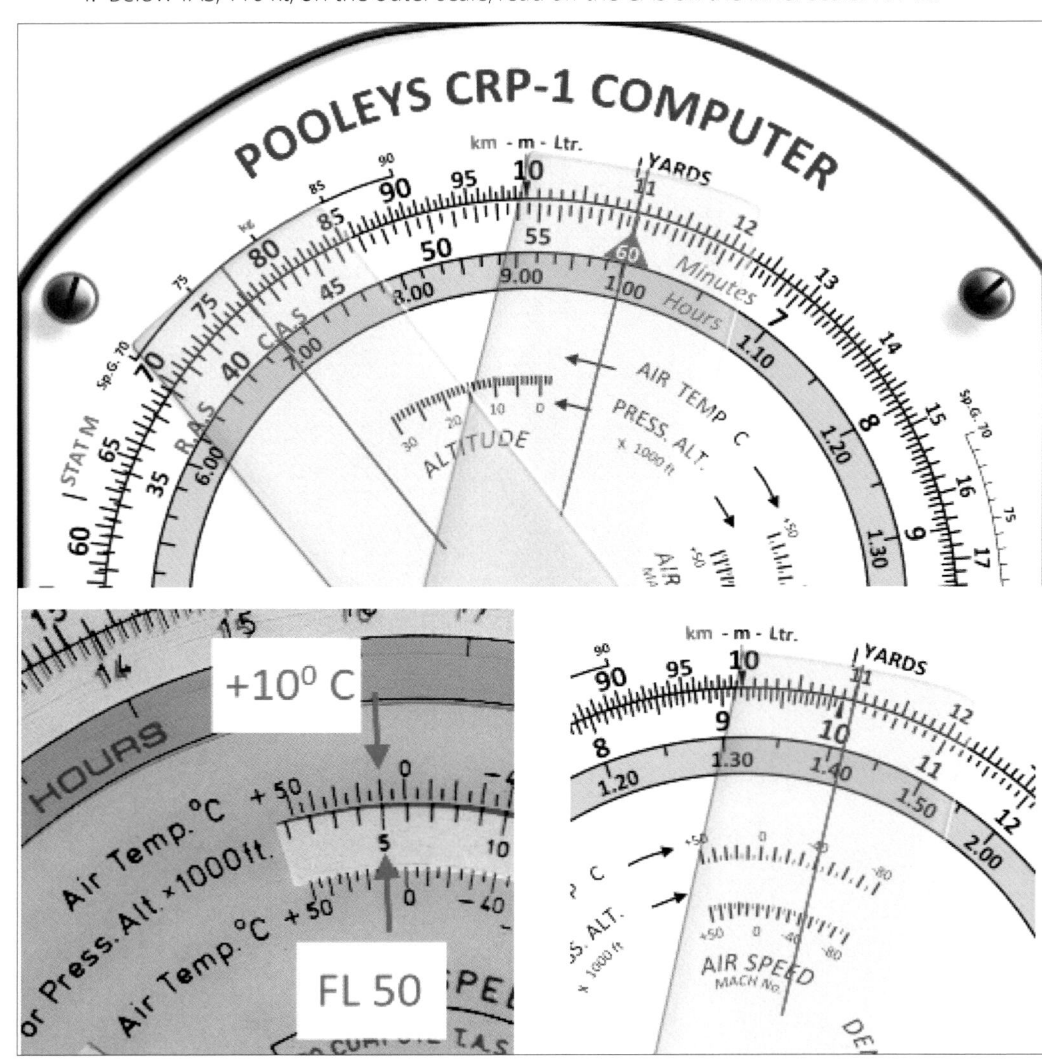

FURTHER READING: APM VOLUME 3, SECTION 2, CHAPTER 10 – TIMING AND FUEL MANAGEMENT

END OF EXPLANATIONS PAPER 2

NAVIGATION: PAPER 3

1. What range is displayed on the DME cockpit display?

a. Slant range
b. Horizontal Range
c. Corrected slant range
d. Arc range

2. Approximately what is the maximum number of aircraft that are able to use a DME station at any one time?

a. 50
b. 75
c. 100
d. 150

3. What is the name of the aircraft equipment needed for secondary surveillance radar?

a. Transmitter
b. Transposer
c. Translator
d. Transponder

4. A Non-Directional Beacon (NDB) is:

a. An airborne system comprising of a loop antenna and a sense antenna
b. A ground based station that radiates two signals out of phase
c. An airborne system to measure the range and bearing from a ground station
d. A ground based station that transmits omni-directionally

5. An aircraft is tracking away from an NDB maintaining a track of 040 with 9° of port drift. What bearing should the relative bearing indicator (RBI) be indicating?

a. 189° relative
b. 180° relative
c. 031° relative
d. 171° relative

6. Parallels of latitude:

a. Are described as being either east or west of 0°
b. Are all small circles, except for the equator
c. Are all great circles
d. Are numbered from 0 to 180

7. With the Sun in the west, the moment when the upper limb of the Sun touches the horizon is known as:

a. Civil twilight
b. Sunrise
c. Dawn
d. Sunset

8. An aircraft is maintaining a compass heading of 315° C, the deviation is 1° E, the true heading is 324° T. What is the magnetic variation?

a. 8° E
b. 10 ° E
c. 10° W
d. 8° W

9. If an aircraft flies due south along the 045° W meridian from latitude 37° N to 21° 45′ S. What distance is covered in i) nautical miles ii) statute miles and iii) kilometres?

a. i) 3,480 nm ii) 4,000 sm iii) 6,440 km
b. i) 3,525 nm ii) 4,055 sm iii) 6,520 km
c. i) 975 nm ii) 1,805 sm iii) 1,120 km
d. i) 3,435 nm ii) 3,950 sm iii) 6,350 km

10. Which of the following navigation aids use frequencies in the VHF band?

a. DME and VOR
b. VOR and VDF
c. GPS, NDB and VDF
d. NDB, VOR and VDF

11. With increasing latitude magnetic dip becomes .... (i) .... and compass errors .... (ii) ....:

a. i. Less ii. Reduce
b. i. Less ii. Increase
c. i. Greater ii. Increase
d. i. Greater ii. Reduce

12. An aircraft is flying between two points 90 nm apart, after 50 nm the aircraft is found to be 7 nm to the left of track. In order to route directly to the destination what heading correction is necessary?

a. 10.5° right
b. 8.4° left
c. 20.1° left
d. 18.9° right

13. The range and accuracy of VHF transmissions are degraded by:

a. The altitude and range of the receiving aircraft, thunderstorm effect and coastal refraction.
b. Site and propagation errors, the altitude and range of the receiving aircraft and the height of the ground based transmitter.
c. Site and propagation errors, night effect and the height of the ground based transmitter.
d. The height of the ground based transmitter, coastal refraction and night effect.

14. Overhead point A the fuel contents are 52 kg. 38 minutes later, over point B, the fuel contents is 45 kg. Your destination, C, is 1 hour and 14 minutes away.

Assuming the fuel flow remains constant and a Specific Gravity (Sp. G) of 0.72, how much fuel will remain, in USG, when overhead C?

a. 31.3 USG
b. 13.7 USG
c. 22.4 USG
d. 11.5 USG

15. An aircraft is flying at an indicated air speed (IAS) of 120 knots at FL 80. The OAT is 11° C greater than the ISA, what is the aircraft's true airspeed (TAS)? Ignore position and instrument errors.

a. 133 kt
b. 138 kt
c. 115 kt
d. 144 kt

16. Complete the table below. From the completed table what is the magnetic heading and duration for the leg?

Pressure Altitude (FT)/ OAT(°C)	CAS (kt)	TAS (kt)	W/V	TR (T)	HDG (T)	Var.	HDG (M)	GS	DIST (NM)	Time
5000/-10	110		360/30	210		5E			79	

a. Magnetic Heading 215°; Duration 34 minutes
b. Magnetic Heading 217°; Duration 36 minutes
c. Magnetic Heading 222°; Duration 34 minutes
d. Magnetic Heading 212°; Duration 34 minutes

17. Given the following details calculate the wind velocity:

TAS	90 knots
GROUNDSPEED	88 knots
TRUE HEADING	322 degrees
TRUE TRACK	310 degrees

a. 260/18
b. 010/20
c. 060/20
d. 040/18

18. Your aircraft is maintaining a TAS of 121 knots and arrives overhead turning point A at 1826 UTC. Turning point B is 48 nm away using a track of 140° T. Calculate your ETA at B using a forecast wind of 200/20 kt.

a. 1848 UTC
b. 1857 UTC
c. 1841 UTC
d. 1852 UTC

19. What is the name given to a line which crosses all meridians at the same angle?

a. A parallel
b. A great circle
c. A rhumb line
d. A grid line

END OF NAVIGATION PAPER 3

NAVIGATION PAPER 3: ANSWERS

No	A	B	C	D
1	X			
2			X	
3				X
4				X
5				X
6		X		
7				X
8	X			
9		X		
10		X		
11			X	
12				X
13		X		
14				X
15		X		
16				X
17				X
18				X
19			X	

CORRECT ANSWERS: PERCENTAGES					
15	16	17	18	19	20
75%	80%	85%	90%	95%	100%

1. **(Answer: A)** Distance Measuring Equipment provides you with the distance of your aircraft from the ground station. It is important to remember that the information given is the slant range; when close to the ground station the information will be at its most inaccurate.

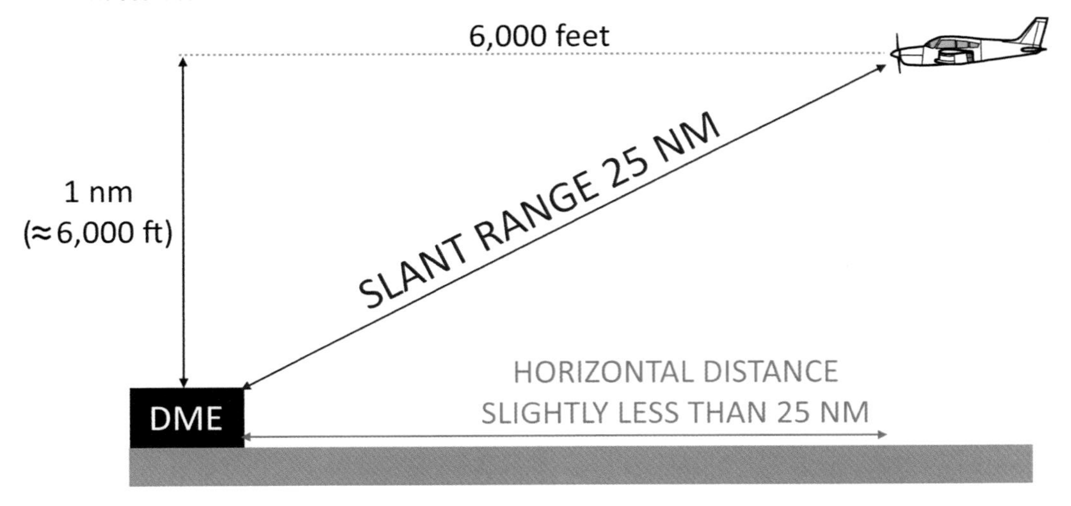

FURTHER READING: APM VOLUME 3, SECTION 4, CHAPTER 21 – DME

2. **(Answer: C)** DME operates by the aircraft equipment (the interrogator) transmitting a coded pulse signal on the selected frequency; the signal reaches the ground station where it is retransmitted. When the retransmitted signal reaches the aircraft the DME equipment recognises its own code and knows that the radio wave has travelled at a fixed speed. The interrogator can therefore work out how long it has taken for the pulse signal to travel to and return from the DME ground station and can calculate the distance.

   There is a practical limit to how many aircraft can use or "lock on" to a DME station at any one time. Most can deal with no more than around 100 aircraft, when this limit is exceeded the ground station will begin to disregard the weaker signals, these will normally be the most distant from the station. Newer DME stations will be able to handle more aircraft.

   DME operates in the UHF band. Each DME channel consists of two frequencies one for the interrogation signal from the aircraft and a separate, but automatically paired, response frequency from the ground station. There are 126 channels classified as either X or Y.

FURTHER READING: APM VOLUME 3, SECTION 4, CHAPTER 21 – DME

3. **(Answer: D)** A transponder is the airborne equipment required in the aircraft for the SSR system operate.

FURTHER READING: APM VOLUME 3, SECTION 4, CHAPTER 18 – RADAR

4. **(Answer: D)** A Non-Directional Beacon (NDB) is the most basic navigation aid. It is a ground station that transmits radio energy in all directions. NDBs operate in the low or medium frequency bands.

The accuracy of an NDB can be seriously reduced by:
Thunderstorm effect: The ADF needle can be deflected towards an electrical storm and away from the ground station.
Night Effect: Strong sky waves can be present in the LF and MF frequency bands especially at dawn and dusk. At these times signals from the beacon can take different paths to the aircraft either by surface wave or sky wave, the two paths interfere with each other, the signal may fade and the needle wander.
Mountain Effect: Where signals from the beacon are reflected by terrain.
Coastal Effect: Caused by the radio wave bending (refracting) when it crosses a coast at an angle.

FURTHER READING: APM VOLUME 3, SECTION 4, CHAPTER 22 – THE NDB AND THE ADF

5. **(Answer: D)** 171° relative

Drift is measured from the heading (nose) to the track, and is classified in degrees port or starboard of heading.

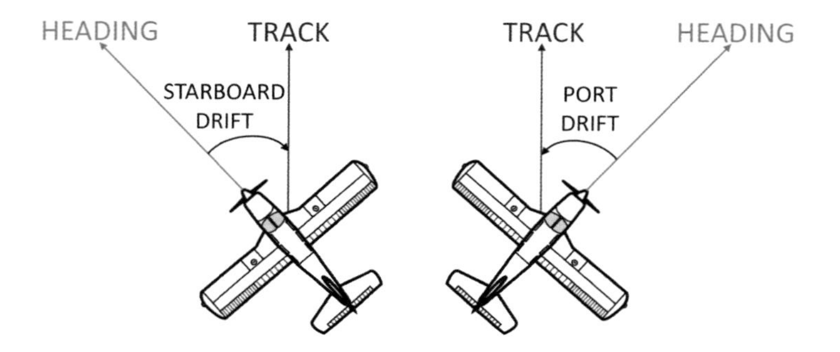

If there were to be no cross wind, when tracking away from the NDB flying the heading as a track would work. The needle would continue to show a steady relative bearing of 180° i.e. it will point to the tail of the aircraft. In cross wind conditions an allowance for drift is necessary.

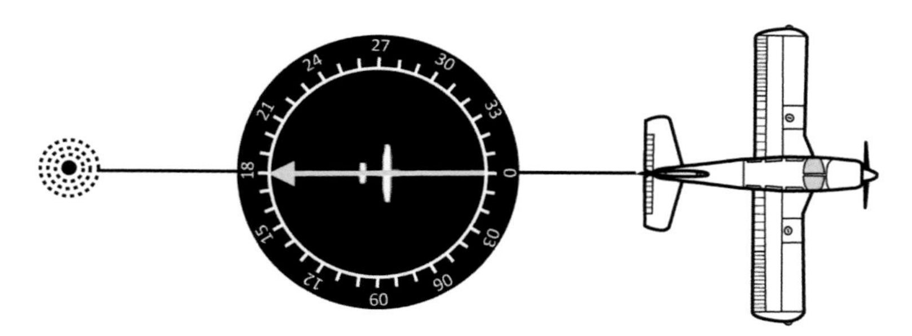

With a track of 040 and a drift 9° to port, the track lies to the left of the heading; therefore the heading is 049°. When using an RBI the "tail" of the ADF needle must be offset 9° I.e. by an equal amount in the opposite direction in order for the desired track to be maintained. To summarise, the aim is to achieve parity between the number of degrees by which the heading is offset in one direction and the number of degrees by which the tail of the ADF needle is displaced in the other direction.

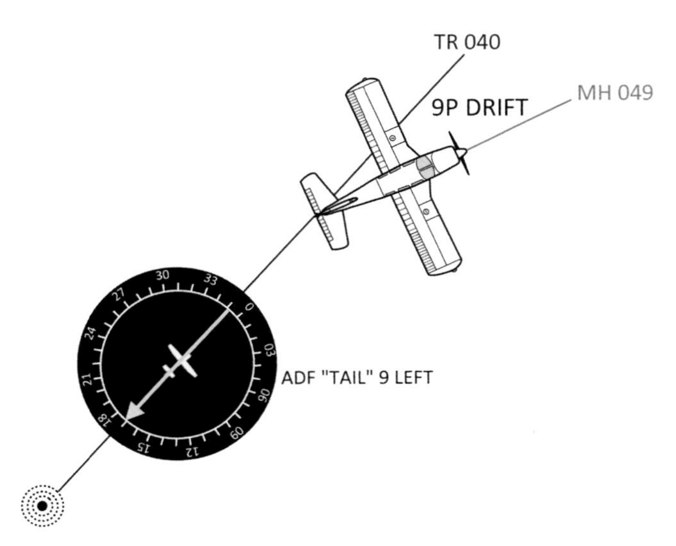

MAGNETIC HEADING + RELATIVE BEARING +/- 180 = QDR
049 + 171 = 220 - 180 = 040

FURTHER READING: APM VOLUME 3, SECTION 4, CHAPTER 22 – THE NDB AND THE ADF

6. **(Answer: B)** All parallels of latitude, except for the equator are small circles. A circle drawn on a sphere whose plane passes exactly through the centre of the sphere itself is called a great circle; the only parallel of latitude that fulfils this criterion is the equator.

FURTHER READING: APM VOLUME 3, SECTION 1, CHAPTER 1 – THE EARTH

7. **(Answer: D)** The Sun moves across the sky from east in the morning to west in the evening. Therefore, in this question the Sun is going down, and it refers to sunset. Sunrise and sunset conventionally refer to the times when the upper limb of the disk of the Sun is on the horizon.

   Civil Twilight:

   In the morning: starts when the centre of the Sun's disc is 6° below the horizon and finishes at sunrise.

   In the evening: starts at sunset and ends when the centre of the Sun's disc is 6° below the horizon.

FURTHER READING: APM VOLUME 3, SECTION 1, CHAPTER 3 – TIME

8. **(Answer: A)** The best way to begin with such questions is to use **T v M d C**, and to create a table containing the known details.

True Heading	Variation	Magnetic Heading	Deviation	Compass Heading
324			1E	315

Remember also "East is Least; West is Best" – meaning that easterly corrections are subtracted and westerly ones added when working from left to right..

True Heading	Variation	Magnetic Heading	Deviation	Compass Heading
324	**8E**	**316**	1E	315

The magnetic variation is 8°E.

FURTHER READING: APM VOLUME 3, SECTION 1, CHAPTER 4 – THE MAGNETIC COMPASS AND DIRECTION

9. **(Answer: B)** A nautical mile is defined as a unit of distance equal to one minute (')of arc on the earth's surface. Each degree of latitude is made up of 60 minutes and therefore equates to 60 nm. As long as the movement is along a great circle, i.e. any meridian or the equator, the conversion between change in latitude and distance is straight forward.

To begin with find the total distance travelled in degrees and minutes. In this case the locations given are in opposite hemispheres and so the latitudes are added together: 37° + 21° 45' = 58° 45'

To find the distance in nm multiply each full degree travelled by 60: 58 x 60 = 3,480 nm
And add any extra minutes: 3,480 + (45 minutes at 1 nm per minute) = 3,525 nm
For this question we now have to convert our answer to statute miles and kilometres:
Mathematically: 1 nm = 1.15 sm = 1.85 km
3,525 x 1.15 = 4,054 sm
3,525 x 1.85 = 6,521 km

CRP 1:

1. Set the nm on the inner rotating scale against "NAUT M" on the outside of the computer, using the guide line to help.
2. The guide line can then be rotated to "STAT M" and the statute miles read off on the inner scale. Here 4,060 sm.
3. The process is then repeated using "km-m –ltr". Reading the inner scale gives 6,510 km.

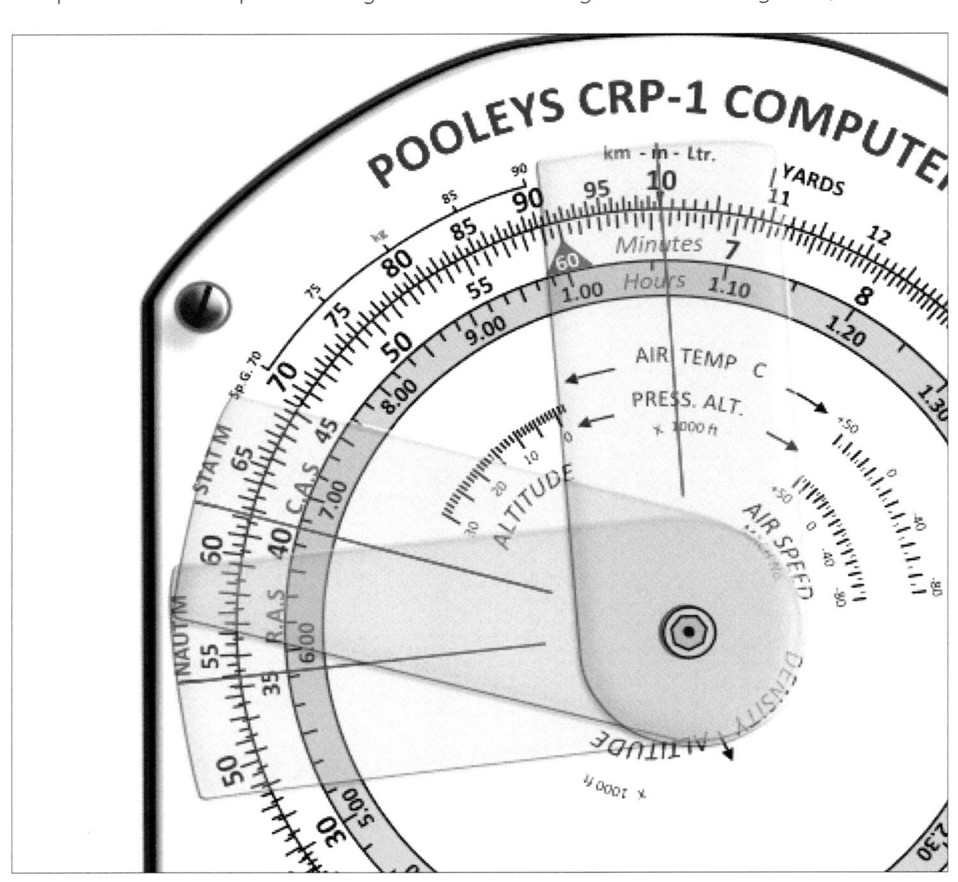

The best fitting answers are: i) 3,525 nm ii) 4,055 sm iii) 6,520 km

FURTHER READING: APM VOLUME 3, SECTION 2, CHAPTER 10 – TIMING AND FUEL MANAGEMENT

10. **(Answer: B)** VOR and VDF operate in the VHF band.

NAV AID	NAV AID	FREQUENCY BAND
DME	Distance Measuring Equipment	UHF
GPS	Global Positioning System	L-band (microwaves)
NDB	Non-Directional Beacon	LF and MF
Radar	Primary Radar	UHF, S-band and L-band depending on range required.
SSR	Secondary Surveillance Radar	UHF
VDF	VHF Direction Finding	VHF
VOR	VHF Omni-directional Range	VHF

FURTHER READING: APM VOLUME 3, SECTION 4, CHAPTER 23 – VHF DIRECTION FINDING (VDF)

11. **(Answer: C)** With increasing latitude magnetic dip becomes greater and compass errors increase.

The compass suffers from both turning and acceleration errors as a result of magnetic dip, or "z", leading to the weight of the magnet not being directly underneath the pivot. Magnetic dip is due to the magnet trying to align itself with the earth's magnetic field which is practically horizontal at the equator, but almost vertical at the poles. Where dip is minimal the compass will be at its most accurate and this will occur at low latitudes. Arranging the magnet as a pendulum does alleviate some of the problem, but will not eradicate it totally.

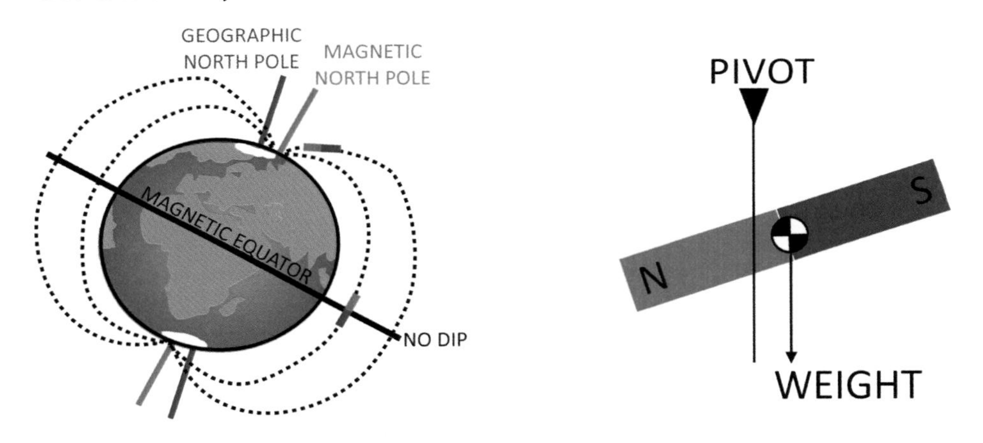

FURTHER READING: APM VOLUME 3, SECTION 1, CHAPTER 4 – THE MAGNETIC COMPASS AND DIRECTION

12. (Answer: D) 18.9° right. Off track errors can be calculated using the "One in Sixty" Rule.

TO FIND TRACK ERROR USING CRP

OUTER SCALE:	DISTANCE OFF TRACK (nm)	TRACK ERROR (degrees)
INNER SCALE:	DISTANCE TRAVELLED (nm)	60

TO FIND CLOSING ANGLE USING CRP

OUTER SCALE:	DISTANCE OFF TRACK (nm)	CLOSING ANGLE (degrees)
INNER SCALE:	DISTANCE TO GO (nm)	60

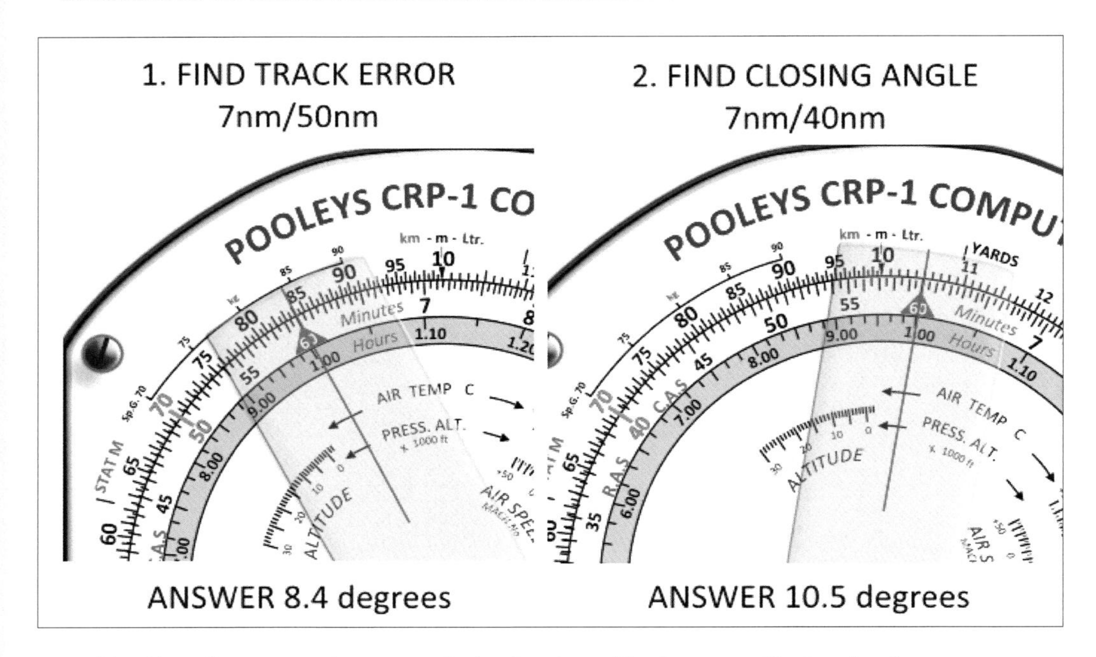

Total heading correction to reach destination = Track error + Closing Angle
= 8.4° + 10.5° = 18.9°

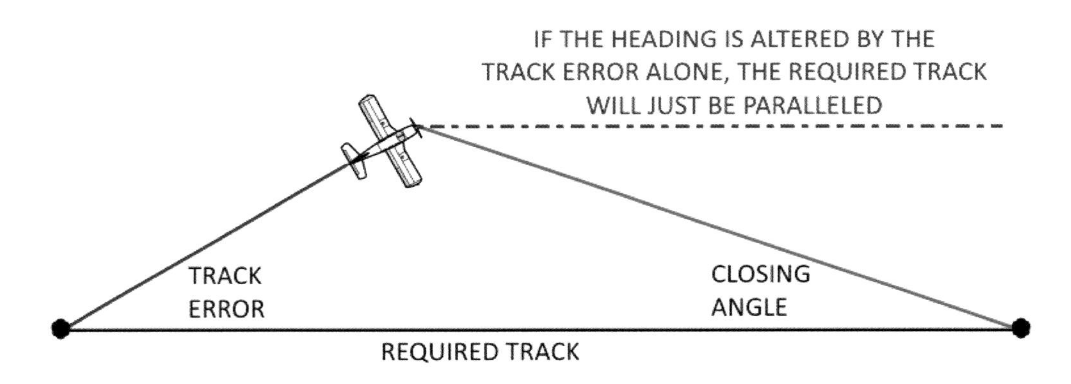

The heading must be corrected 18.9° right.

FURTHER READING: APM VOLUME 3, SECTION 3, CHAPTER 12 – ENROUTE NAVIGATION TECHNIQUES

13. **(Answer: B)** The range and accuracy of VHF transmissions may be degraded by:

- Site and propagation errors,
- The altitude and range of the receiving aircraft and
- The height of the ground based transmitter

Site errors are caused by reflections from buildings, uneven ground etc.. and propagation errors by the radio wave scalloping over differing terrain, these are particularly noticeable at long range from the transmitter.

The other issues are due to the fact that VHF transmissions are line of sight.

Coastal refraction, night errors and thunderstorm effect have an influence in the lower frequency bands, MF and LF, and could degrade the performance of transmissions from an NDB.

FURTHER READING: APM VOLUME 3, SECTION 4, CHAPTER 23 – VHF DIRECTION FINDING (VDF)

14. **(Answer: D)** 11.5 USG.

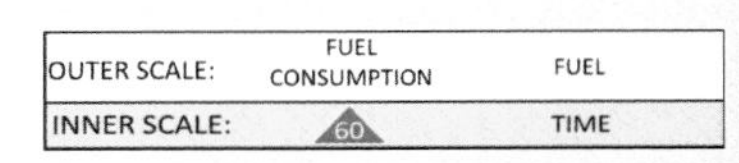

OUTER SCALE:	FUEL CONSUMPTION	FUEL
INNER SCALE:	60	TIME

Using the CRP-1 to find fuel consumption:

1. Set time elapsed between A and B, 38 minutes under the fuel used (52 – 45 = 7 kg)
2. Read fuel consumption above the time index

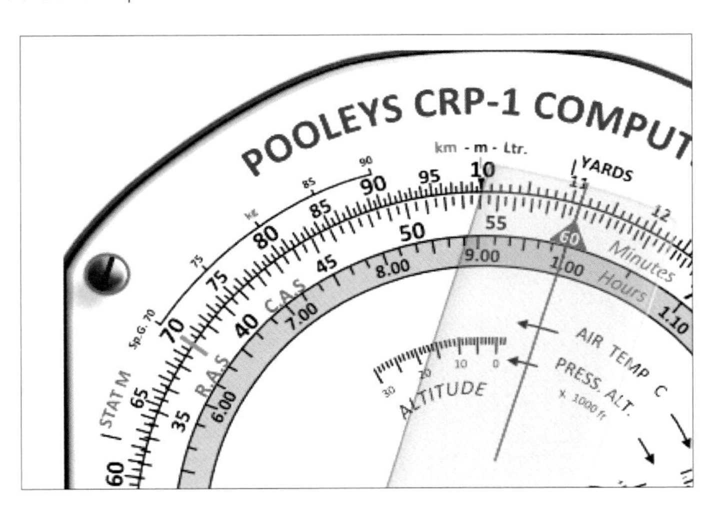

Fuel flow 11.1 kg/hr

Fuel required to reach C:

3. Keep the CRP as it is, i.e. with your calculated fuel consumption above the index
4. The next leg will take 74 minutes, find 74 on the inner rotating scale and read off the fuel required above on the outer scale.

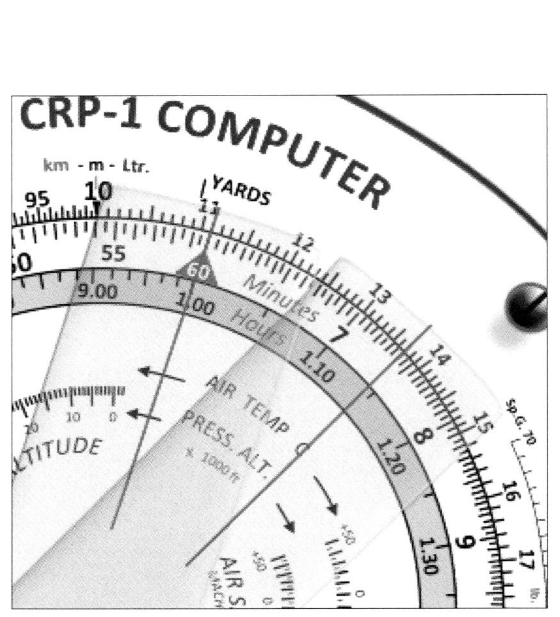

Fuel required: 13.7 kg.

Therefore overhead C the remaining fuel will be: 45 – 13.7 = 31.3 kg

To find USG remaining:

5. Set the guide line to 0.72 on the Sp.G scale for kg (be careful – there is a scale in lb as well!)
6. Below the guide line on the inner rotating scale set the weight of fuel, 31.3 kg
7. Reset the guide line to the USG index
8. Read off the USG equivalent on the inner scale

11.5 USG.

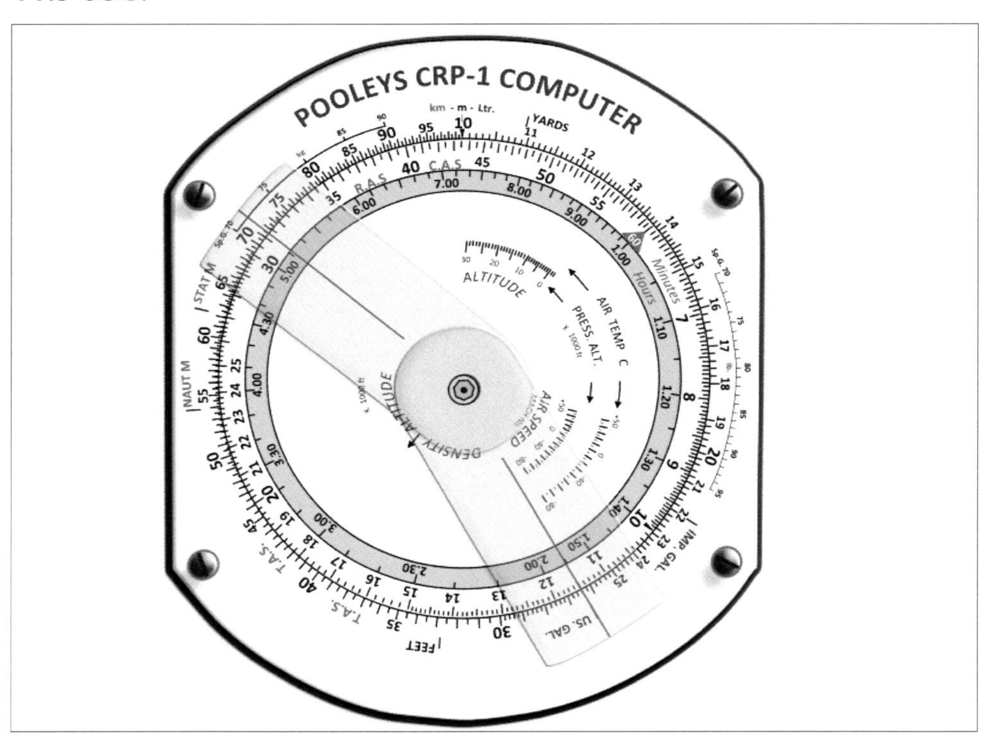

FURTHER READING: APM VOLUME 3, SECTION 2, CHAPTER 10 – TIMING AND FUEL MANAGEMENT

15. (Answer: B) 138 kt.

The first stage is to calculate the OAT. The ISA assumes the temperature at ground level to be +15°C, and the lapse rate of 2°C reduction in temperature per 1000 ft of height increase.

At FL 80 in a standard atmosphere the temperature will be +15 – (8 x 2) = -1° C
We are told that the OAT is 11° C greater than the ISA, and therefore must be +10° C.

1. In the AIRSPEED window, align the OAT with the pressure altitude.

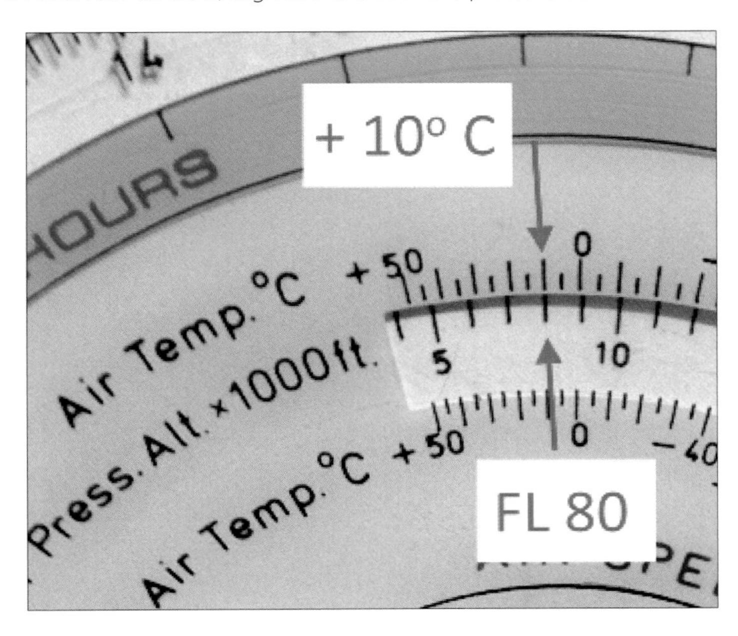

2. Find the IAS on the inner rotating scale. It is now possible to read off the TAS on the outer scale above.

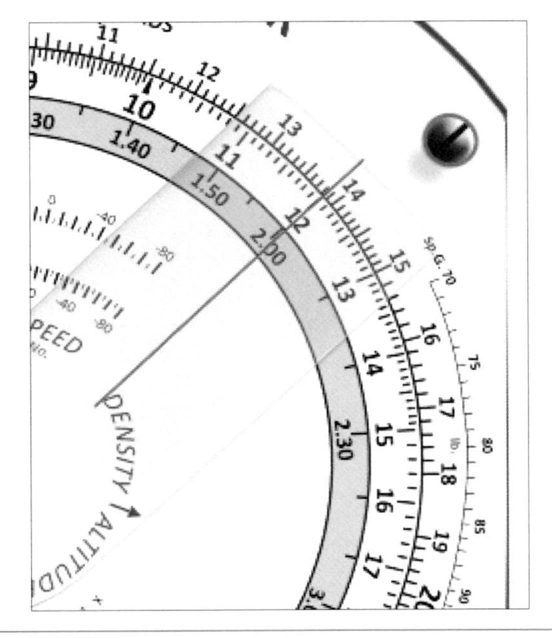

FURTHER READING: APM VOLUME 3, SECTION 2, CHAPTER 8 – AIRSPEED

16. (Answer: D) Magnetic Heading 212°; Duration 34 minutes.

Pressure Altitude (FT)/ OAT(°C)	CAS (kt)	TAS (kt)	W/V	TR (T)	HDG (T)	Var.	HDG (M)	GS	DIST (NM)	Time
5000/-10	110	**115**	360/30	210	**217**	5E	**212**	**141**	79	**34**

The first step is to find the TAS. Using your CRP flight computer, in the AIRSPEED window, align the OAT (-10° C) with the pressure altitude (5000 ft); find the CAS (110 kt) on the inner rotating scale and read off the TAS above it on the outer scale above.

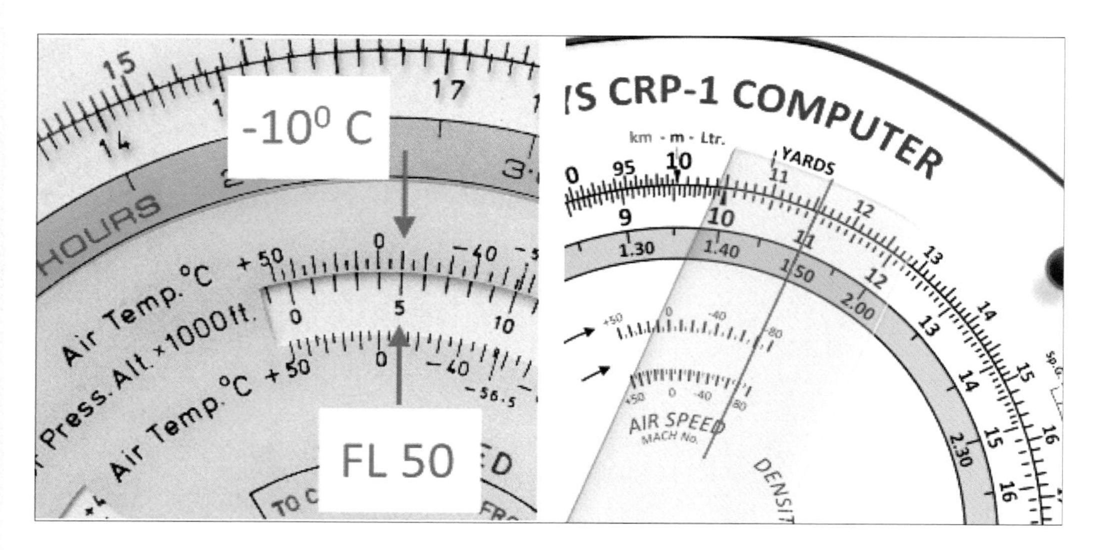

Next, find the magnetic heading:

1. Set the wind direction (360) on the rotating inner scale under the Index on the fixed outer scale.
2. Set the centre circle on a convenient speed arc – 100 is a handy round number. Mark down the wind speed, 30 knots for this question.
3. Move the sliding scale so that the centre circle is over the TAS 115.
4. Rotate the inner scale so that the measured true track, 210, is now below the index. Note the wind mark is now displaced 6° to the left.
5. Rotate the inner scale 6° to the left, 210 is now below 6° on the left hand side of the fixed drift scale. However, now the wind dot indicates 7° of port drift. What we are aiming for is parity, so move the rotating scale so that 210 is below 7° on the fixed drift scale and still left of the index. We have parity – the track is offset 7° and the wind mark still shows 7°.
6. Read off the true heading under the Index = 217°.
7. Apply the variation, in this case 5° E. Remember "East is Least, West is Best", the variation is West, hence here we subtract it giving a magnetic heading of 212°.
8. Finally, before putting the CRP away note the ground speed = 141 kt.

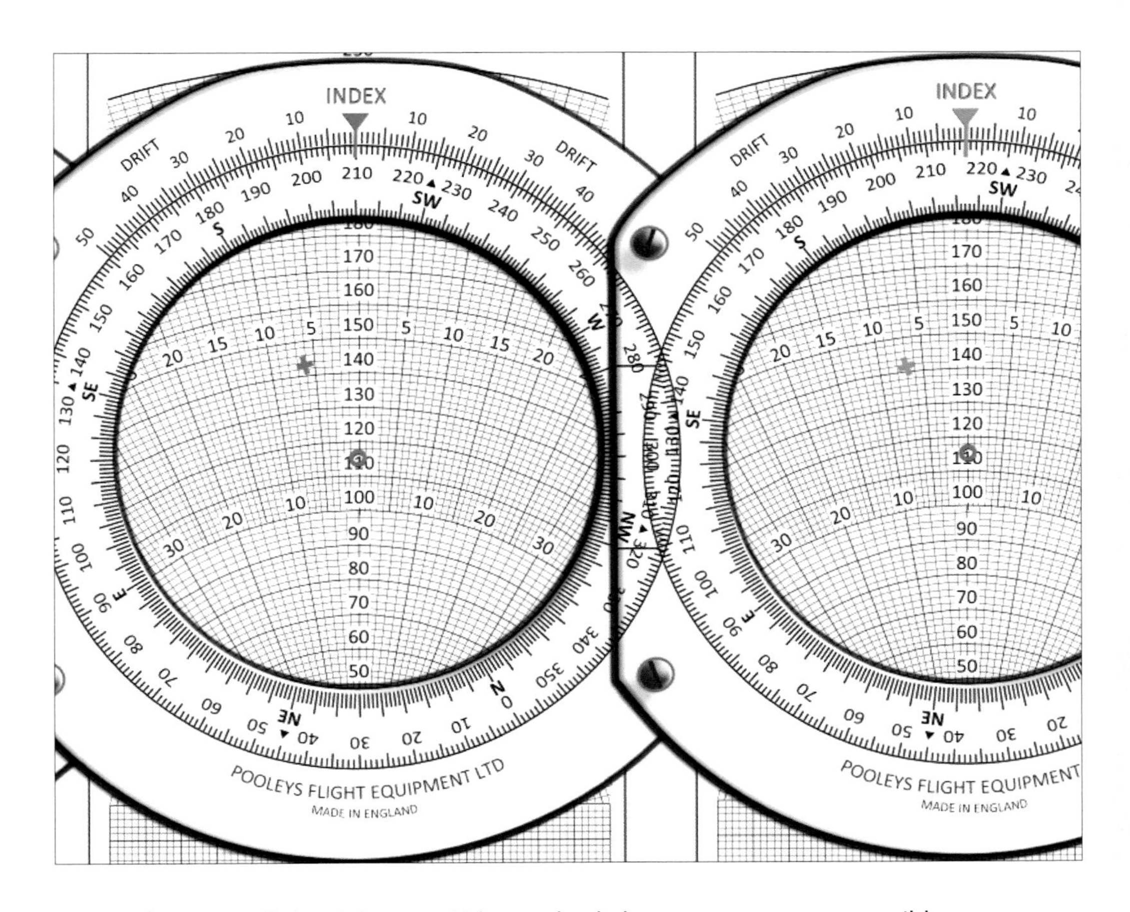

Making a small sketch is a good idea to check that your answers are sensible:

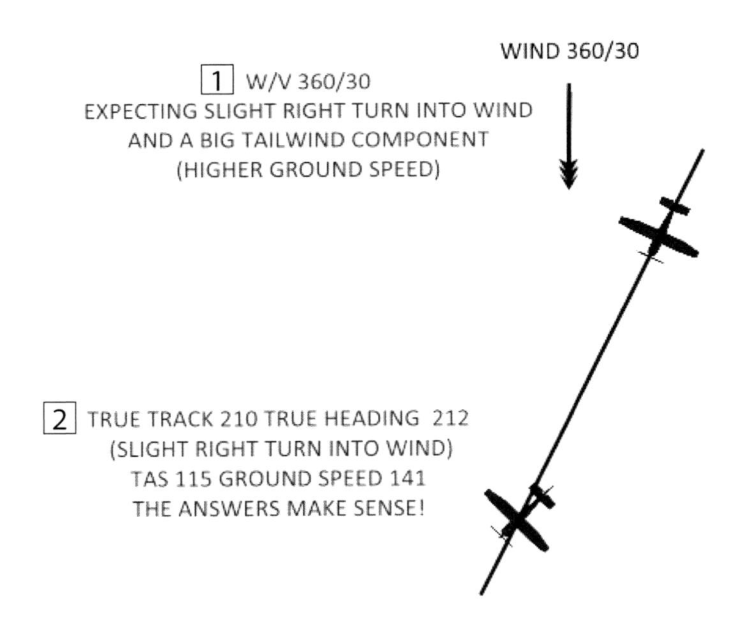

Lastly, we are asked to find the time it will take to fly the leg:

OUTER SCALE:	DISTANCE	SPEED
INNER SCALE:	TIME	60

Again, it is useful to have an idea of the answer we are expecting to get so that we can be confident that we have read the computer correctly. Very roughly a ground speed of 141 knots is close to 150, which would give us a rate over the ground of just under 2.5 nm per minute. The distance, 79 nm, divided by 2.5 gives an answer of 31.6, so we are anticipating an answer just over 30 minutes.

Back to the CRP, set the "60" mark on the rotating inner scale under the ground speed, here 141 knots. Re-set the moving lubber line to 79 nm (the distance) on the outer scale – here it helps to remember from school "speed = distance over time" i.e. distance is set on the outer scale OVER time on the inner.

Read off the time on the top of the inner scale 34 minutes.

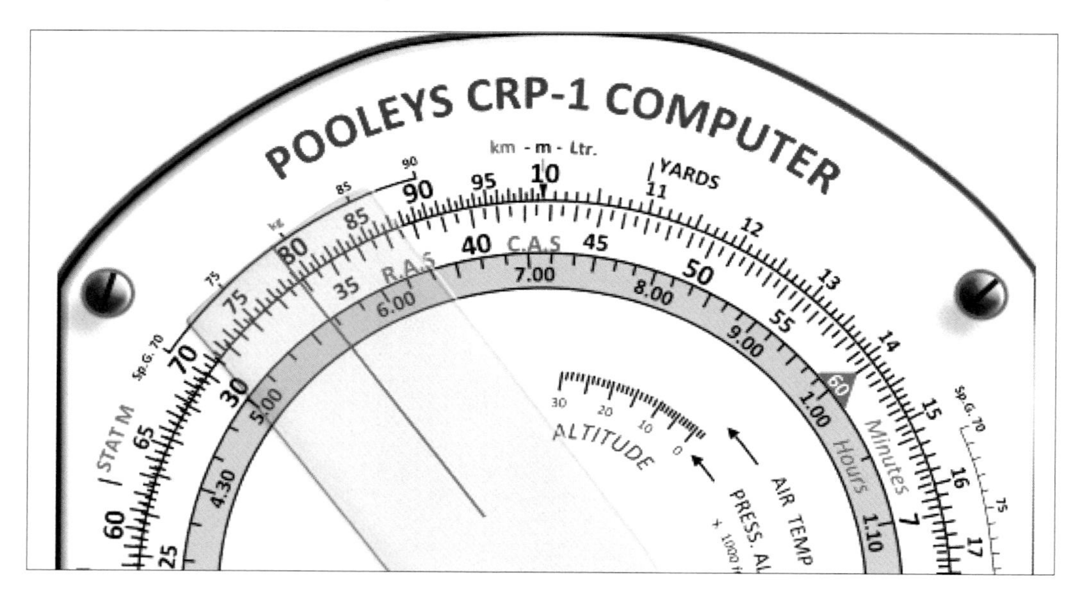

FURTHER READING: APM VOLUME 3, SECTION 2, CHAPTER 9 – DRIFT

17. (Answer: D) 040/18.

1. Place centre dot on TAS, 90 knots
2. Set Heading, 322, under the index
3. The difference between heading and track is 12°. It is port drift as the track is to the left of the heading

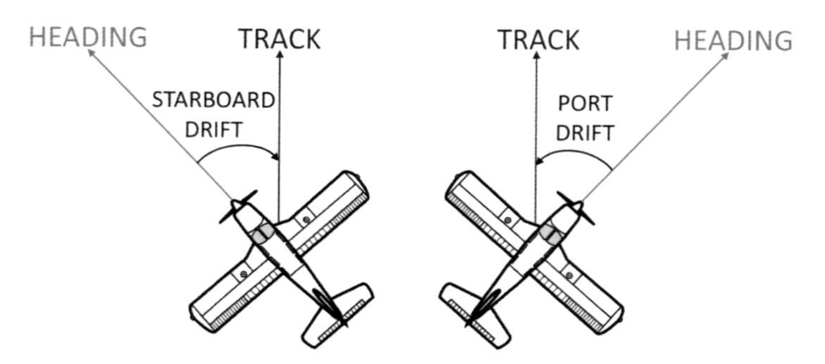

4. Follow the arc representing the groundspeed, 88 knots, and make a mark to represent the drift - 12° right
5. Now, move the centre dot down to the wind component grid.
6. Rotate the inner disc until your wind mark is below the centre dot.

7. Read off the wind direction under the index, 036 degrees and the velocity under the mark on the wind component grid, here 22 knots.

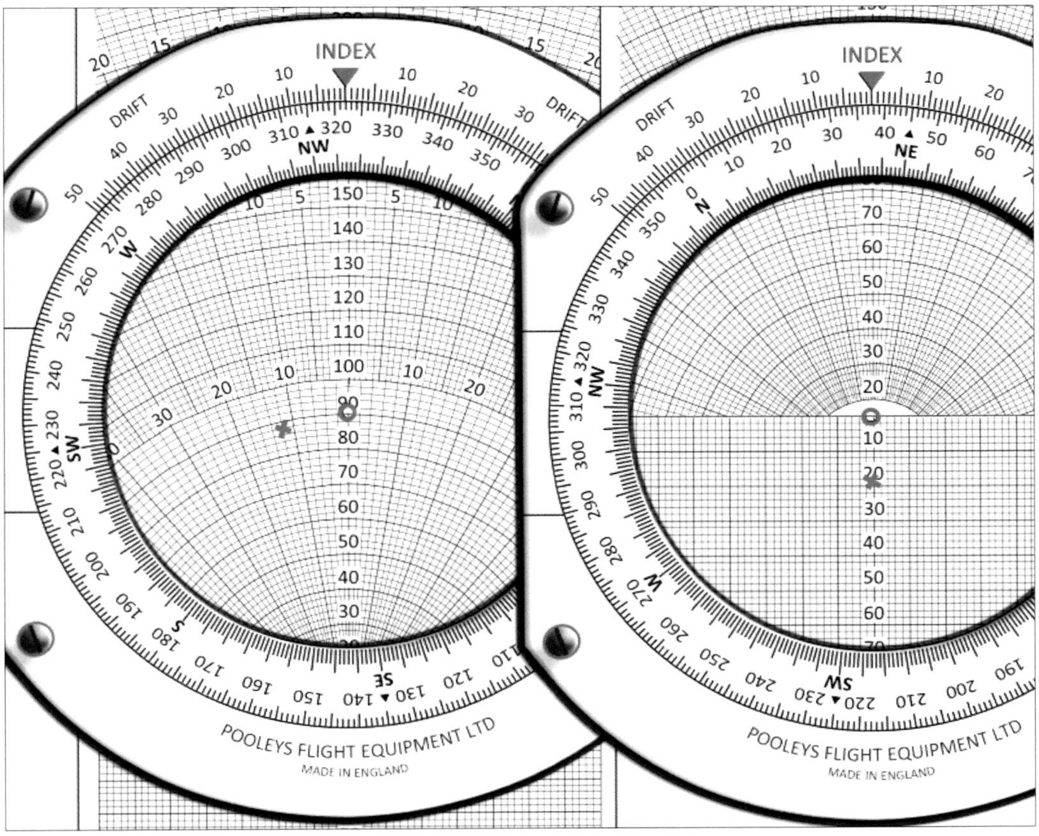

Closest answer 040/18.

Carry out a "common sense" check, with a wind of 040/18 kt and a track of 310, you would expect to turn right into wind (heading 322 achieves this), and we would expect little change in groundspeed due to a mainly crosswind component. The answer we obtained therefore seems sensible.

FURTHER READING: APM VOLUME 3, SECTION 2, CHAPTER 9 – DRIFT

18. (Answer: D) 1852 UTC.

To begin with find the ground speed:

1. Set the wind direction (200) on the rotating inner scale under the Index on the fixed outer scale.
2. Set the centre circle on a convenient speed arc – 100 is a handy round number. Mark down the wind speed, 20 knots for this question.
3. Move the sliding scale so that the centre circle is over the TAS 121.
4. Rotate the inner scale so that the measured true track, 140, is now below the index.
5. Read off the ground speed: 113 kt

Carry out a common sense check: The difference between the heading 140 and the wind direction 200 is 60°, and we can see from the CRP that it is a headwind and can anticipate a groundspeed lower than the TAS.

20 x 0.5 = 10 knots

121 – 10 = 111 knots ground speed

OUTER SCALE:	DISTANCE	SPEED
INNER SCALE:	TIME	60

Rule of Thumb:

The cross wind component can be roughly calculated using the sine of number of degrees between the heading (or runway direction) and the wind direction. Similarly the cosine of that angle can be used to find a head or tailwind component.

SINE	CROSSWIND COMPONENT
30° = 0.5	50% of wind speed
40° = 0.6	60% of wind speed
50° = 0.7	70% of wind speed
60° = 0.9	90% of wind speed

COSINE	HEAD/TAIL WIND COMPONENT
30° = 0.9	90% of wind speed
40° = 0.75	75% of wind speed
50° = 0.6	60% of wind speed
60° = 0.5	50% of wind speed

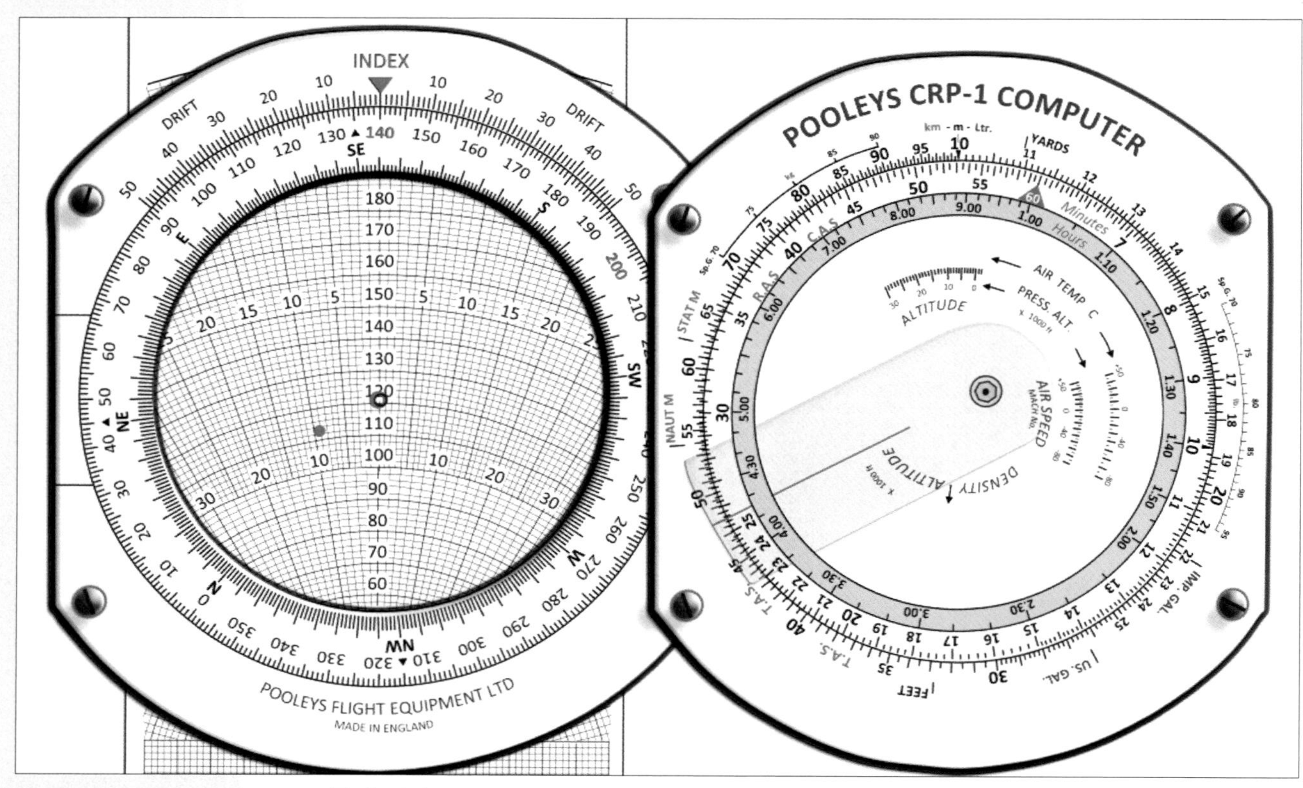

To find the time to point B:

1. Place the ground speed, 113 kt, over the time index
2. On the outer scale find the distance 48 nm
3. Read off the time on the inner scale: 25.5 minutes
4. Again a common sense check shows that if we are travelling at nearly 2 nm per minute (120 kts): 48 ÷ 2 = 24 minutes

Finally, add your result to the time to find the ETA: 1826 + 25.5 = 1851.5 UTC

Closest answer 1852 UTC.

FURTHER READING: APM VOLUME 3, SECTION 2, CHAPTER 9 – DRIFT

19. **(Answer: C)** A rhumb line is a line which crosses all meridians of longitude at the same angle.

- A straight line drawn on a Transverse Mercator projection is a rhumb line.
- All parallels of latitude are rhumb lines, since they intersect with the meridians at the same angle.
- As a constant angle is maintained a rhumb line is easier to fly

FURTHER READING: APM VOLUME 3, SECTION 1, CHAPTER 2 – AERONAUTICAL CHARTS

END OF EXPLANATIONS PAPER 3

NAVIGATION: PAPER 4

1. You are flying towards a VOR on the 255 radial. In order to obtain CDI indications in the correct sense the OBS should be set to:
   - **a.** 075° with a TO indication
   - **b.** 255° with a FROM indication
   - **c.** 255° with a TO indication
   - **d.** 075° with a FROM indication

2. An aircraft is tracking away from an NDB maintaining a track of 300° with 5° of starboard drift. What bearing should the relative bearing indicator (RBI) indicate?
   - **a.** 185° relative
   - **b.** 180° relative
   - **c.** 175° relative
   - **d.** 300° relative

3. An aircraft is tracking towards an NDB maintaining a track of 270° with 8° of port drift. What bearing should the relative bearing indicator (RBI) indicate?
   - **a.** 008° relative
   - **b.** 360° relative
   - **c.** 270° relative
   - **d.** 352° relative

4. A QDM is:
   - **a.** Magnetic bearing of the aircraft from the VDF station
   - **b.** Magnetic heading (in nil wind) to steer to reach the VDF station
   - **c.** True bearing of the aircraft from the VDF station
   - **d.** True heading (in nil wind) to steer to reach the VDF station

5. An aircraft is tracking away from an NDB maintaining a track of 090 with 8° of port drift. What bearing should the relative bearing indicator (RBI) indicate?
   - **a.** 180° relative
   - **b.** 188° relative
   - **c.** 172° relative
   - **d.** 099° relative

6. When using a chart constructed on Lambert projection:
   - **a.** Meridians of longitude are straight lines, parallels of latitude are curved lines convex towards the nearest pole
   - **b.** Both meridians and parallels are straight lines
   - **c.** Meridians of longitude are straight lines, parallels of latitude are curved lines concave towards the nearest pole
   - **d.** Meridians of longitude are curved lines, parallels of latitude are straight lines

7. Civil Twilight in the evening is from:
   - **a.** When the centre of the Sun's disc is 6° below the horizon to sunset
   - **b.** Sunset and ends when the centre of the Sun's disc is 6° below the horizon
   - **c.** When the centre of the Sun's disc is 6° below the horizon to sunrise
   - **d.** Sunrise and ends when the centre of the Sun's disc is 6° below the horizon

8. You are flying and maintaining a heading of 179° C with 11° right drift. From the compass card you know that the deviation is 4° W, the magnetic variation in the area is 9°W. What is the aircraft's true track?

a. 177° T
b. 166° T
c. 192° T
d. 190° T

9. If an aircraft flies due north along a meridian from latitude 05° 30′ S to 32° 30′ N. In kilometres what distance is covered?

a. 2,620 km
b. 1,620 km
c. 4,230 km
d. 4,280 km

10. The VOR receiver displays:

a. A true bearing to the VOR
b. A magnetic bearing relative to the VOR station
c. The slant distance to the VOR station
d. A compass bearing relative to the VOR station

11. The angle between the Earth's magnetic field and the horizontal is referred to as:

a. Deviation
b. Variation
c. Slip (or "z")
d. Dip (or "z")

12. An aircraft is flying between two points 140 nm apart, after 40 nm the aircraft is found to be 2 nm to the left of track. In order to route directly to the destination what heading correction is necessary?

a. 4.2° right
b. 3° right
c. 4.2° left
d. 3° left

13. Magnetic dip may be defined as:

a. The angle between a magnetic needle in a compass and the horizontal
b. The angle between true and magnetic north
c. The angle between compass heading and magnetic north
d. The angle between the magnetic compass needle and true north

14. The fuel tanks on an aircraft contain 40 litres, with a fuel flow of 9 USG per hour, how long will it take to exhaust the tanks completely?

a. 1 hour 52 minutes
b. 1 hour 10 minutes
c. 2 hours 16 minutes
d. 44 minutes

15. An aircraft is flying at an indicated air speed (IAS) of 92 knots at FL 60. The OAT is 17° C greater than the ISA, what is the aircraft's true airspeed (TAS)? Ignore position and instrument errors.

a. 95 kt
b. 111 kt
c. 122 kt
d. 104 kt

16. Complete the table below. From the completed table what is the magnetic heading and duration for the leg?

Pressure Altitude (FT)/ OAT(°C)	CAS (kt)	TAS (kt)	W/V	TR (T)	HDG (T)	Var.	HDG (M)	GS	DIST (NM)	Time
6000/+20	90		220/30	230		4W			42	

a. Magnetic Heading 223°; Duration 35 minutes
b. Magnetic Heading 231°; Duration 35 minutes
c. Magnetic Heading 237°; Duration 21 minutes
d. Magnetic Heading 232°; Duration 22 minutes

17. Given the following details calculate the wind velocity:

TAS	110 knots
GROUNDSPEED	78 knots
TRUE HEADING	260 degrees
TRUE TRACK	245 degrees

a. 340/35
b. 240/30
c. 110/40
d. 290/40

18. Your aircraft is maintaining a TAS of 110 knots and arrives overhead turning point A at 0812 UTC. Turning point B is 83 nm away using a track of 180° T. Calculate your ETA at B using a forecast wind of 150/40 kt.

a. 0907 UTC
b. 0916 UTC
c. 0846 UTC
d. 0857 UTC

19. A rhumb line may be defined as:

a. A line on the Earth which represents the shortest distance between any two places
b. A line joining places of equal magnetic variation
c. Any line drawn on a chart using a Lambert projection
d. A line on the Earth which crosses all meridians at the same angle

END OF NAVIGATION PAPER 4

NAVIGATION PAPER 4: ANSWERS

No	A	B	C	D
1	X			
2	X			
3				X
4		X		
5			X	
6			X	
7		X		
8	X			
9			X	
10		X		
11				X
12	X			
13	X			
14		X		
15				X
16		X		
17				X
18		X		
19				X

CORRECT ANSWERS: PERCENTAGES					
15	16	17	18	19	20
75%	80%	85%	90%	95%	100%

1. **(Answer: A)** In this question we are told that the aircraft is on the 255 radial, i.e. it is to the west of the beacon. In order to fly to the beacon with correct sense indications the OBS should be set to 075 with a TO indication.

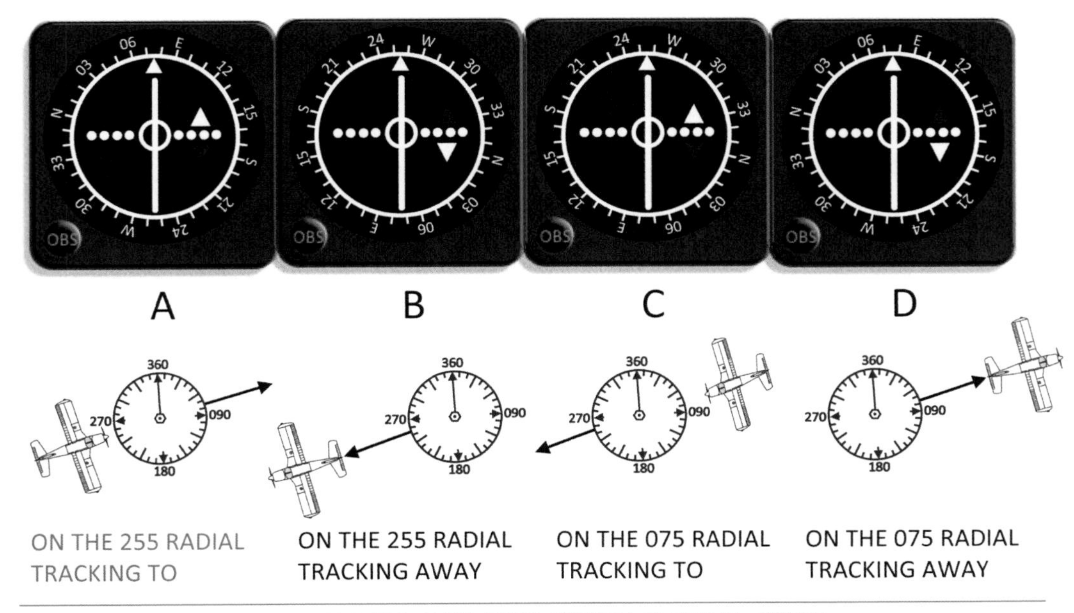

FURTHER READING: APM VOLUME 3, SECTION 4, CHAPTER 20 – THE VOR

2. **(Answer: A)** 185° relative. Drift is measured from the heading (nose) to the track, and is classified in degrees port or starboard of heading.

If there were to be no cross wind, when tracking away from the NDB, flying the heading as a track would work. The needle would continue to show a steady relative bearing of 180° i.e. it will point to the tail of the aircraft.

In cross wind conditions an allowance for drift is necessary.

With a track of 300 and a drift 5° to starboard, the track lies to the right of the heading; therefore the heading is 305°. When using an RBI the "tail" of the ADF needle must be offset 5° right: an equal amount but to the opposite side of the nose in order for the track to be maintained.

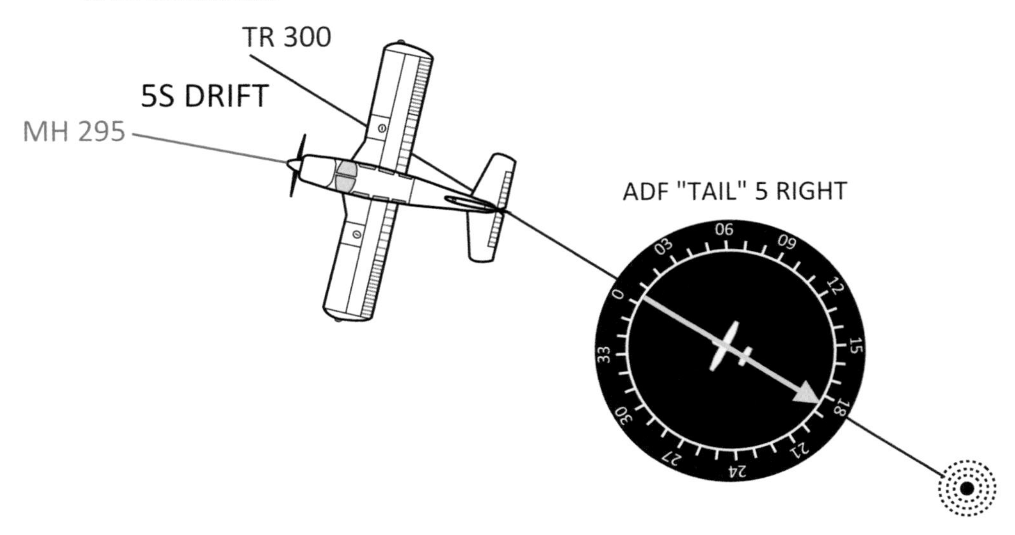

MAGNETIC HEADING + RELATIVE BEARING +/- 180 = QDR

295 + 185 = 480 - 180 = 300

To summarise, when tracking away from an NDB the aim is to achieve parity between the number of degrees by which the heading is offset in one direction and the number of degrees by which the tail of the ADF needle is displaced in the other direction.

FURTHER READING: APM VOLUME 3, SECTION 4, CHAPTER 22 – THE NDB AND THE ADF

3. **(Answer: D)** 352° relative. When tracking towards an NDB in nil wind, the RBI would indicate 000° relative, the needle would point directly to the nose. With 8° of port drift the heading is right of track, the RBI should therefore point 8° left of the nose.

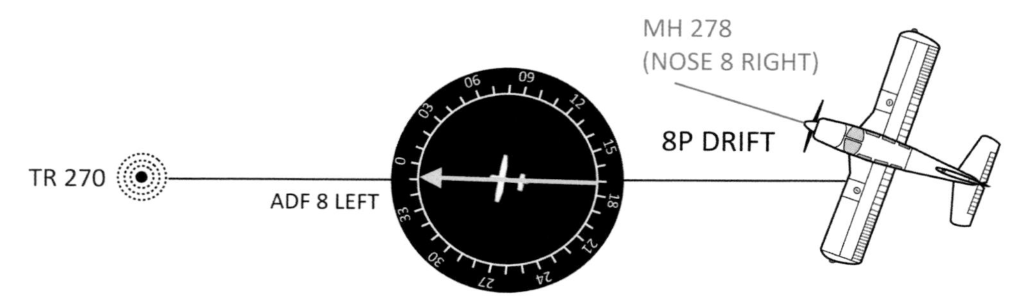

TRACKING TOWARDS THE NDB:
MAGNETIC HEADING + RELATIVE BEARING = QDR
278 + 352 = 630 - 360 = 270

FURTHER READING: APM VOLUME 3, SECTION 4, CHAPTER 22 – THE NDB AND THE ADF

4. **(Answer: B)**

QDM Aircraft's magnetic heading to steer in zero wind to reach the station
QDR Aircraft's magnetic bearing from the station
QTE Aircraft's true bearing from the station
QUJ Aircraft's true track to the station

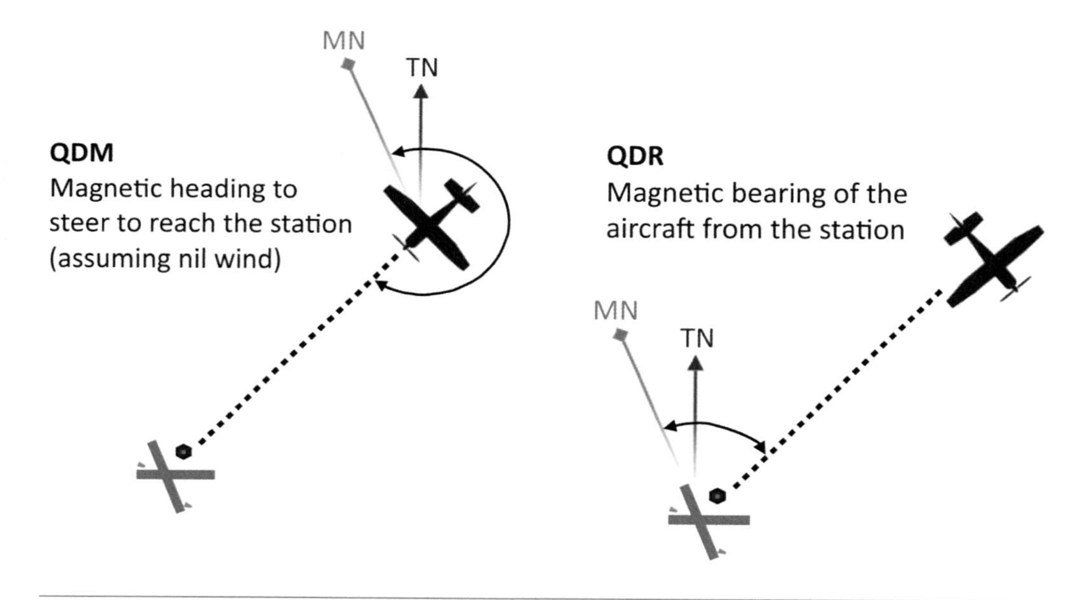

FURTHER READING: APM VOLUME 3, SECTION 4, CHAPTER 22 – THE NDB AND THE ADF

5. **(Answer: C)** 172° relative.

With a track of 090 and a drift 8° to port, the track lies to the left of the heading; therefore the heading is 098°. When using an RBI the "tail" of the ADF needle must be offset 8° left - an equal amount but to the opposite side of the nose in order for the QDR to be maintained.

To summarise, when tracking away from an NDB the aim is to achieve parity between the number of degrees by which the heading is offset in one direction and the number of degrees by which the tail of the ADF needle is displaced in the other direction.

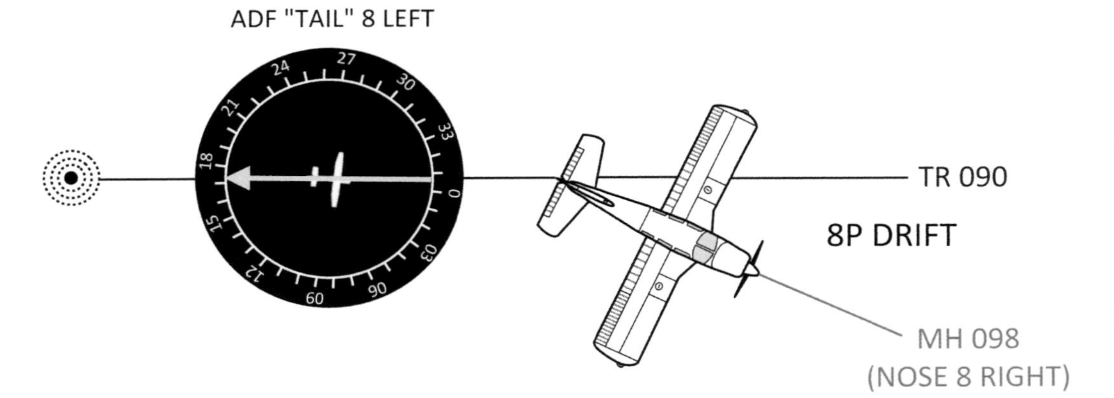

TRACKING AWAY FROM THE NDB
MAGNETIC HEADING + RELATIVE BEARING +/- 180 = QDR
098 + 172 = 270 - 180 = 090

FURTHER READING: APM VOLUME 3, SECTION 4, CHAPTER 22 – THE NDB AND THE ADF

6. **(Answer: C)** On a Lambert projection meridians of longitude appear as straight lines converging towards the poles. Parallels of latitude appear as slightly curved lines, concave towards the nearest pole.

FURTHER READING: APM VOLUME 3, SECTION 1, CHAPTER 1 – EARTH

7. **(Answer: B)** Civil Twilight: In the evening: starts at sunset and ends when the centre of the Sun's disc is 6° below the horizon.

In the morning: starts when the centre of the Sun's disc is 6° below the horizon and finishes at sunrise.

FURTHER READING: APM VOLUME 3, SECTION 1, CHAPTER 3 – TIME

8. **(Answer: A)** The best way to begin with such questions is to use **T v M d C**, and to create a table containing the known details.

True Heading	Variation	Magnetic Heading	Deviation	Compass Heading
	9W		4W	179

Remember also "East is Least; West is Best" – meaning that easterly corrections are subtracted and westerly ones added when working from left to right. It is now possible to complete the table.

True Heading	Variation	Magnetic Heading	Deviation	Compass Heading
166	9W	175	4W	179
Check left to right: 166	166 + 9	175	175 + 4	179

The questions actually asks for the true track, not heading, and so now we must take into account the drift. Drift is measured from the heading (nose) to the track, and is classified in degrees port or starboard of heading.

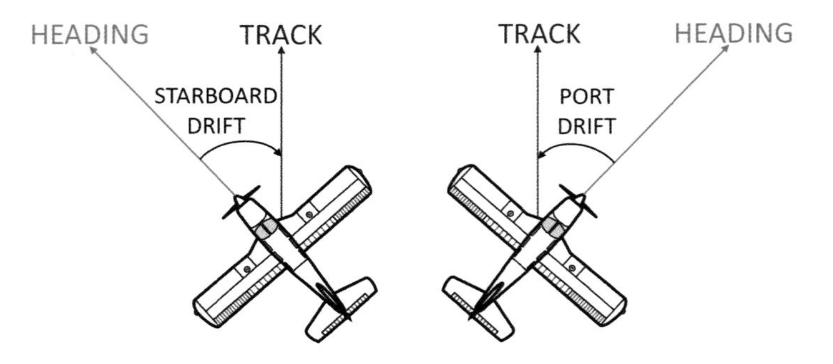

The aircraft is heading 166° T with 11° of right (starboard) drift, therefore the true track is:
166 + 11 = 177° T

FURTHER READING: APM VOLUME 3, SECTION 1, CHAPTER 4 – THE MAGNETIC COMPASS AND DIRECTION

9. **(Answer: C)** A nautical mile is defined as a unit of distance equal to one minute (')of arc on the earth's surface. Each degree of latitude is made up of 60 minutes and therefore equates to 60 nm. As long as the movement is along a great circle, i.e. any meridian or the equator, the conversion between change in latitude and distance is straight forward.

To begin with find the total distance travelled in degrees and minutes. In this case the locations given are in opposite hemispheres and so the latitudes are added together:
05° 30′ + 32° 30′ = 38°

To find the distance in nm multiply each full degree travelled by 60: 38 x 60 = 2,280 nm

For this question we now have to convert our answer to kilometres:
Mathematically: 1 nm = 1.15 sm = 1.85 km
2,280 x 1.85 = 4,218 km

CRP 1:
1. Set the nm on the inner rotating scale against "NAUT M" on the outside of the computer, using the guide line to help.
2. The guide line can then be rotated to "km-m –ltr" and the answer in kilometres read off on the inner scale: 4,240 km

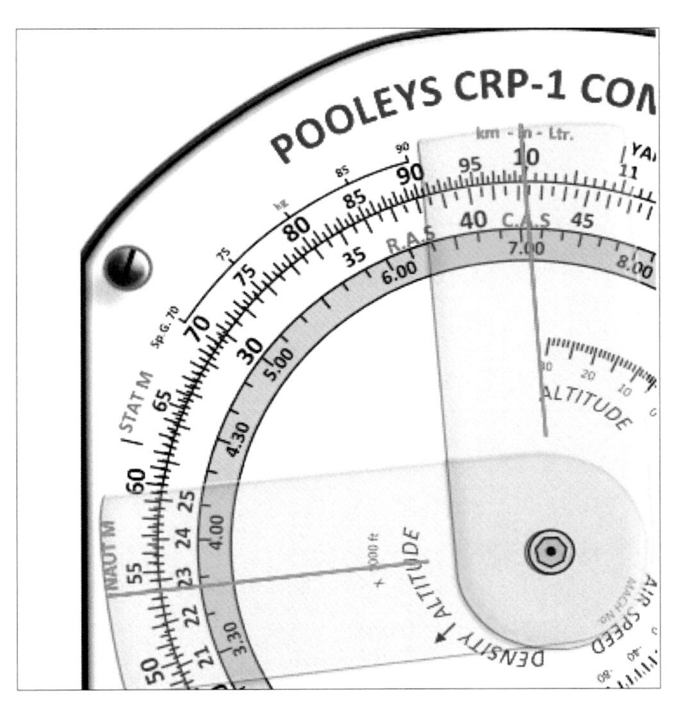

The best fitting answer: **4,230 km.**

FURTHER READING: APM VOLUME 3, SECTION 2, CHAPTER 10 – DRIFT

10. **(Answer: B)** A VOR receiver displays the magnetic bearing from the station, also known as a radial. A radial can also be thought of as a track away from a VOR beacon. The 360 tracks away from a VOR are separated from each other by 1° and are each related to magnetic north. A radial may also be called a QDR.

FURTHER READING: APM VOLUME 3, SECTION 4, CHAPTER 20 – THE VOR

11. **(Answer: D)** Dip, or "z", is the angle between the Earth's magnetic field and the horizontal. Magnetic dip is caused by the magnets in a compass trying to align with the Earth's magnetic field which is practically horizontal at the equator, but almost vertical at the poles.

FURTHER READING: APM VOLUME 3, SECTION 1, CHAPTER 4 – THE MAGNETIC COMPASS AND DIRECTION

12. **(Answer: A)** 4.2° right. Off track errors can be calculated using the "One in Sixty" Rule.

TO FIND TRACK ERROR USING CRP

OUTER SCALE: DISTANCE OFF TRACK (nm)	TRACK ERROR (degrees)
INNER SCALE: DISTANCE TRAVELLED (nm)	60

TO FIND CLOSING ANGLE USING CRP

OUTER SCALE: DISTANCE OFF TRACK (nm)	CLOSING ANGLE (degrees)
INNER SCALE: DISTANCE TO GO (nm)	60

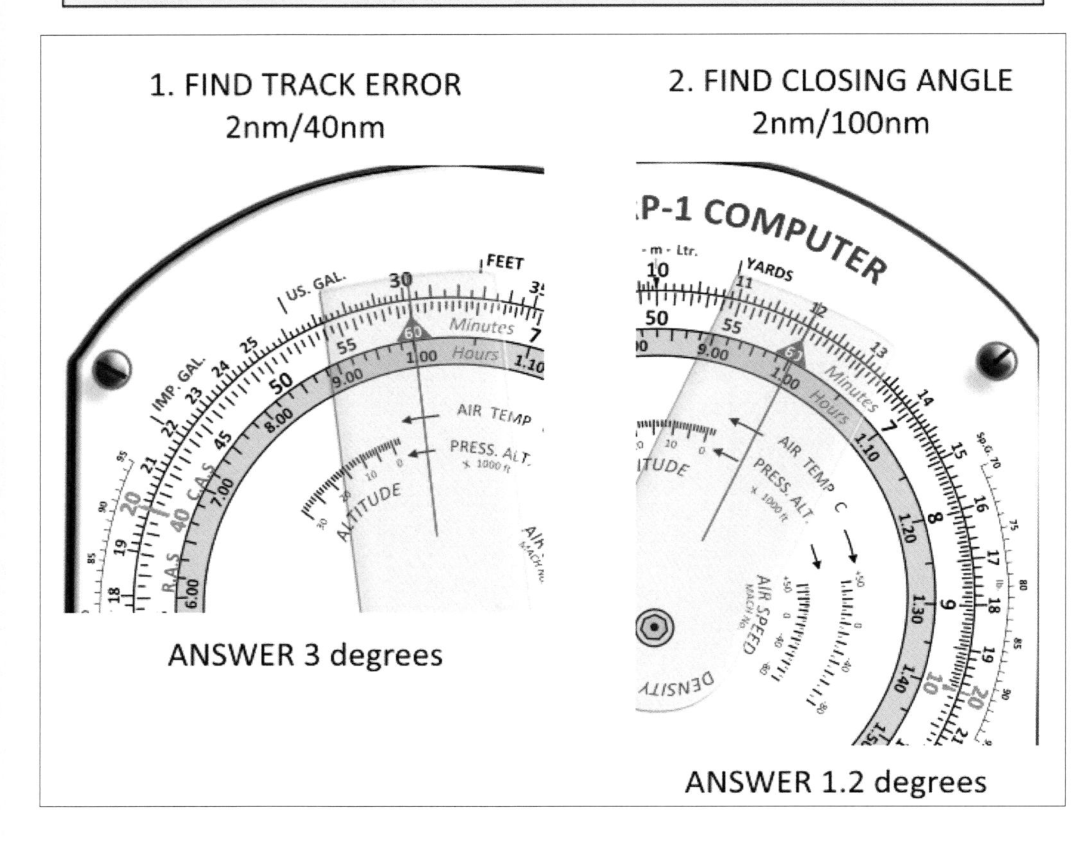

Total heading correction to reach destination = Track error + Closing Angle
= 3° + 1.2° = 4.2°

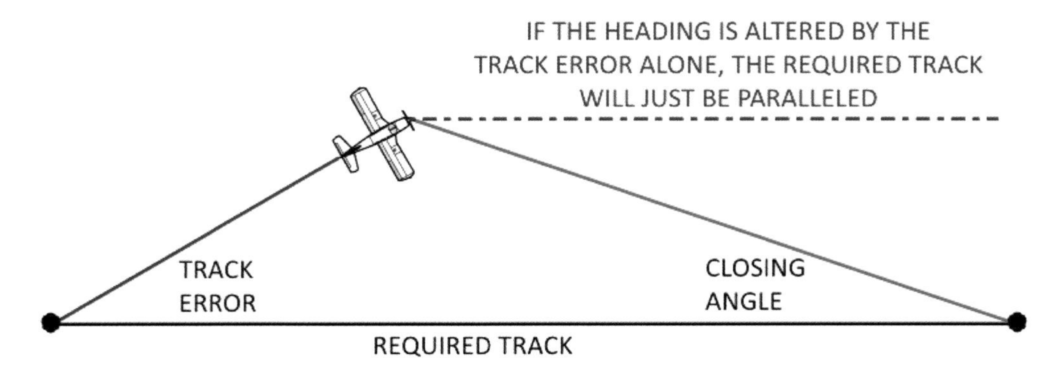

The heading must be corrected 4.2° right.

FURTHER READING: APM VOLUME 3, SECTION 3, CHAPTER 12 – ENROUTE NAVIGATION TECHNIQUES

13. **(Answer: A)** Magnetic dip, or "z", is the angle between the magnetic compass needle and the horizontal. Magnetic dip is caused by the magnets in a compass trying to align with the Earth's magnetic field which is practically horizontal at the equator, but almost vertical at the poles.

FURTHER READING: APM VOLUME 3, SECTION 1, CHAPTER 4 – THE MAGNETIC COMPASS AND DIRECTION

14. **(Answer: B)** 1 hour and 10 minutes

Using your CRP flight computer:

1. Convert the fuel flow into litres. Below the USG index, set the fuel flow – 9 USG.
2. Read off the fuel flow in litres below the km-m-lt index and read off the fuel flow in litres on the inner scale = 34 lt/hr.

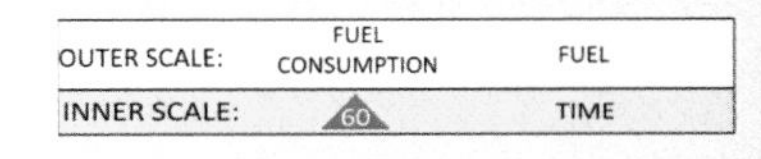

OUTER SCALE:	FUEL CONSUMPTION	FUEL
INNER SCALE:	60	TIME

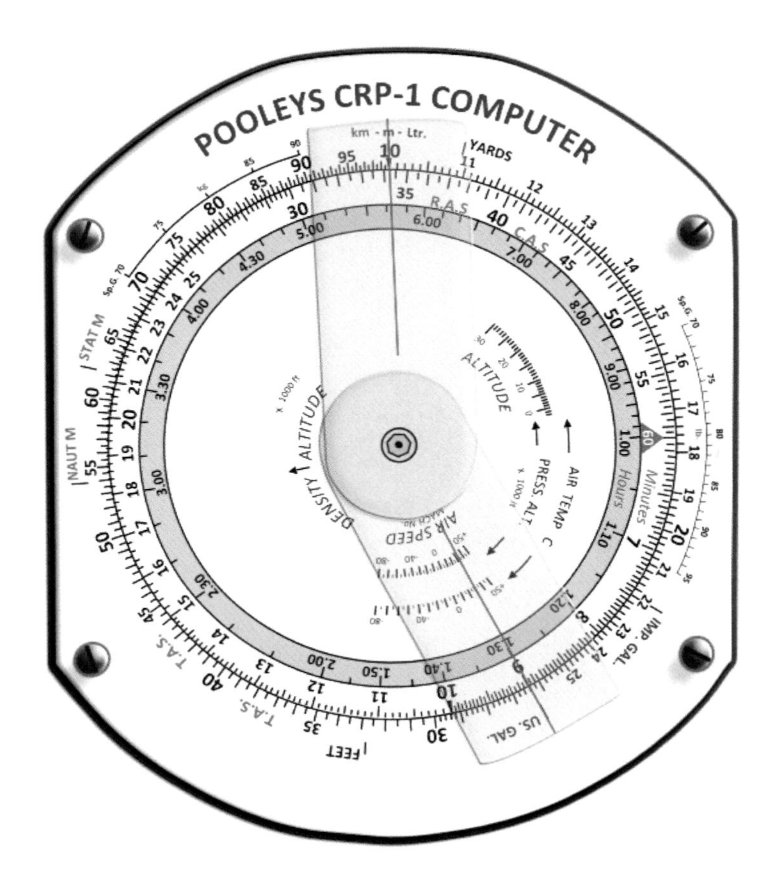

3. Set the fuel flow in litres, 34 lt/hr, above the index.
4. Find the amount of fuel, 40 litres, on the outer scale and read off the time on the inner scale,

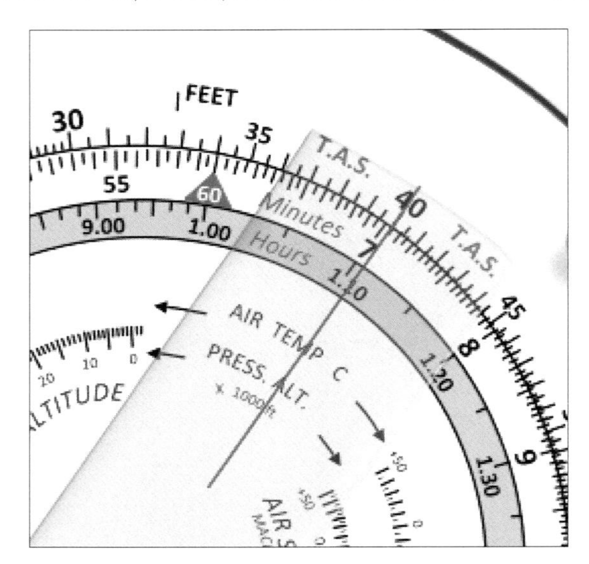

70 minutes or 1 hour and 10 minutes.

FURTHER READING: APM VOLUME 3, SECTION 2, CHAPTER 10 – TIMING AND FUEL MANAGEMENT

15. **(Answer: D)** 104 kt.

The first stage is to calculate the OAT. The ISA assumes the temperature at ground level to be +15°C, and the lapse rate of 2°C reduction in temperature per 1000 ft of height increase.

At FL 60 in a standard atmosphere the temperature will be +15 – (6 x 2) = +3° C
We are told that the OAT is 17° C greater than the ISA, and therefore must be +20° C.

1. In the AIRSPEED window, align the OAT with the pressure altitude.

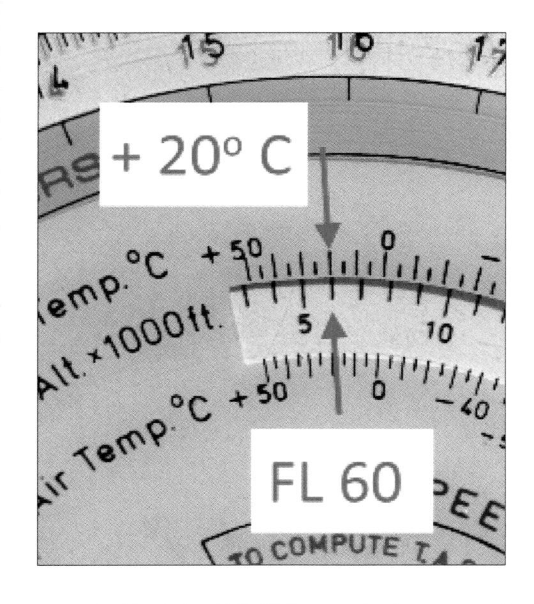

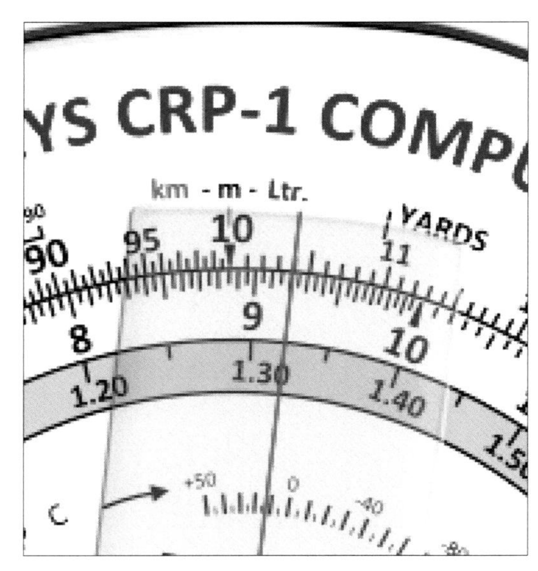

2. Find the IAS, 92 kt, on the inner rotating scale. It is now possible to read off the TAS on the outer scale above .

FURTHER READING: APM VOLUME 3, SECTION 2, CHAPTER 10 – TIMING AND FUEL MANAGEMENT

16. (Answer: B) Magnetic Heading 231°; Duration 35 minutes.

Pressure Altitude (FT)/ OAT(°C)	CAS (kt)	TAS (kt)	W/V	TR (T)	HDG (T)	Var.	HDG (M)	GS	DIST (NM)	Time
6000/+20	90	**102**	220/30	230	**227**	4W	**231**	**73**	42	**35**

The first step is to find the TAS. Using your CRP flight computer, in the AIRSPEED window, align the OAT (+20° C) with the pressure altitude (6000 ft); find the CAS (90 kt) on the inner rotating scale and read off the TAS above it on the outer scale above.

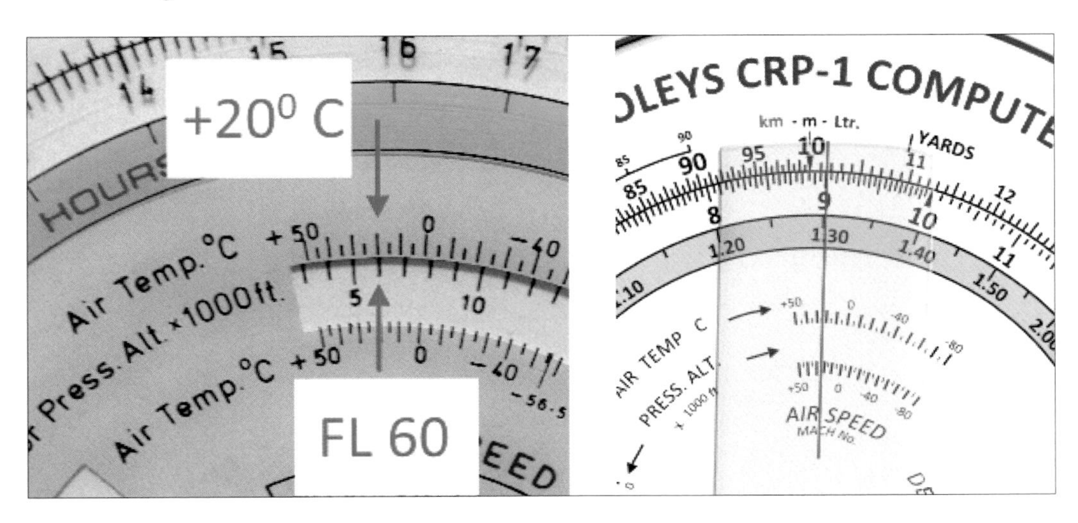

Next, find the magnetic heading:

1. Set the wind direction (220) on the rotating inner scale under the Index on the fixed outer scale.
2. Set the centre circle on a convenient speed arc – 100 is a handy round number. Mark down the wind speed, 30 knots for this question.
3. Move the sliding scale so that the centre circle is over the TAS 102.
4. Rotate the inner scale so that the measured true track, 230, is now below the index. Note the wind mark is now displaced 4° to the right.
5. Rotate the inner scale 4° to the right, 230 is now below 4° on the right hand side of the fixed drift scale. However, now the wind dot indicates 3° of starboard drift. What we are aiming for is parity, so move the rotating scale so that 230 is below 3° on the fixed drift scale and still right of the index. We have parity – the track is offset 3° and the wind mark still shows 3°.
6. Read off the true heading under the Index = 227°.
7. Apply the variation, in this case 4° W. Remember "East is Least, West is Best", the variation is West, hence here we add it giving a magnetic heading of 231°.
8. Finally, before putting the CRP away note the ground speed = 73 kt

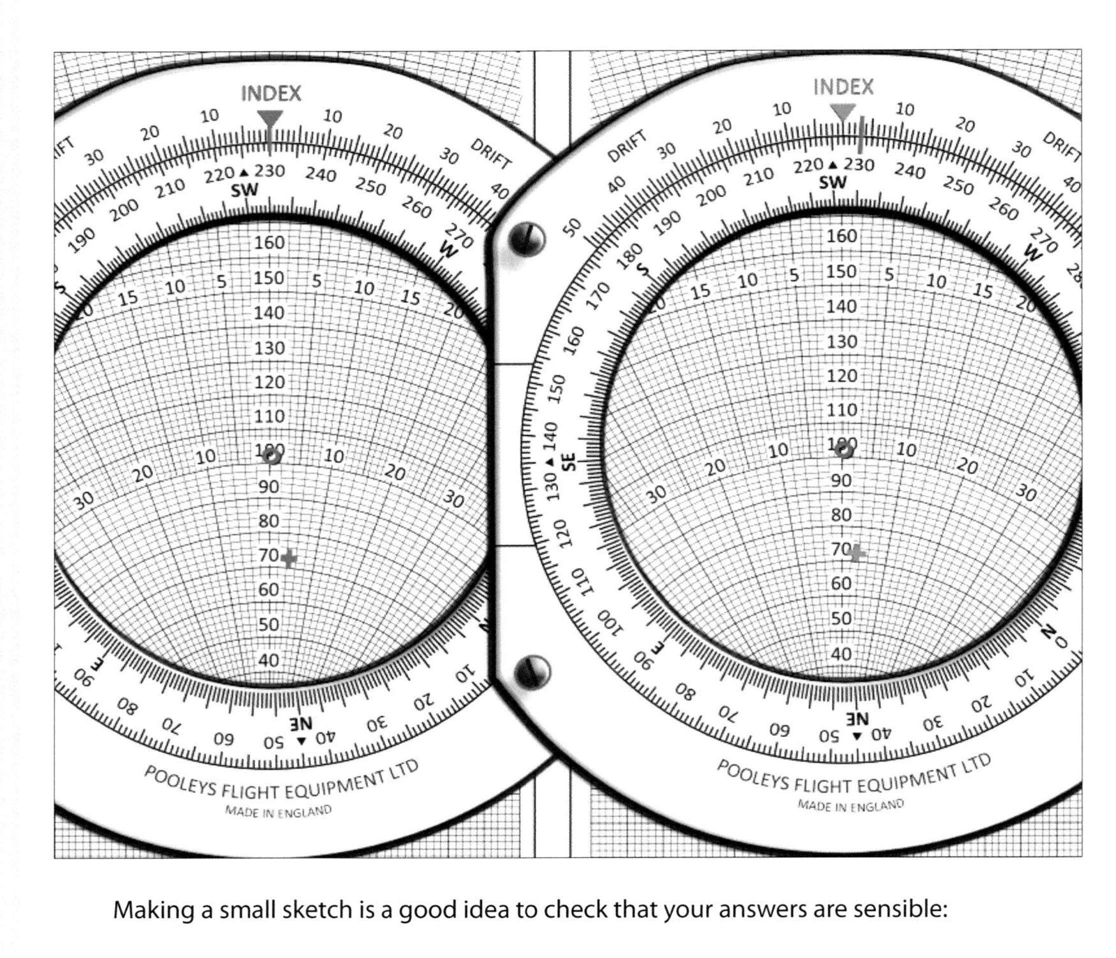

Making a small sketch is a good idea to check that your answers are sensible:

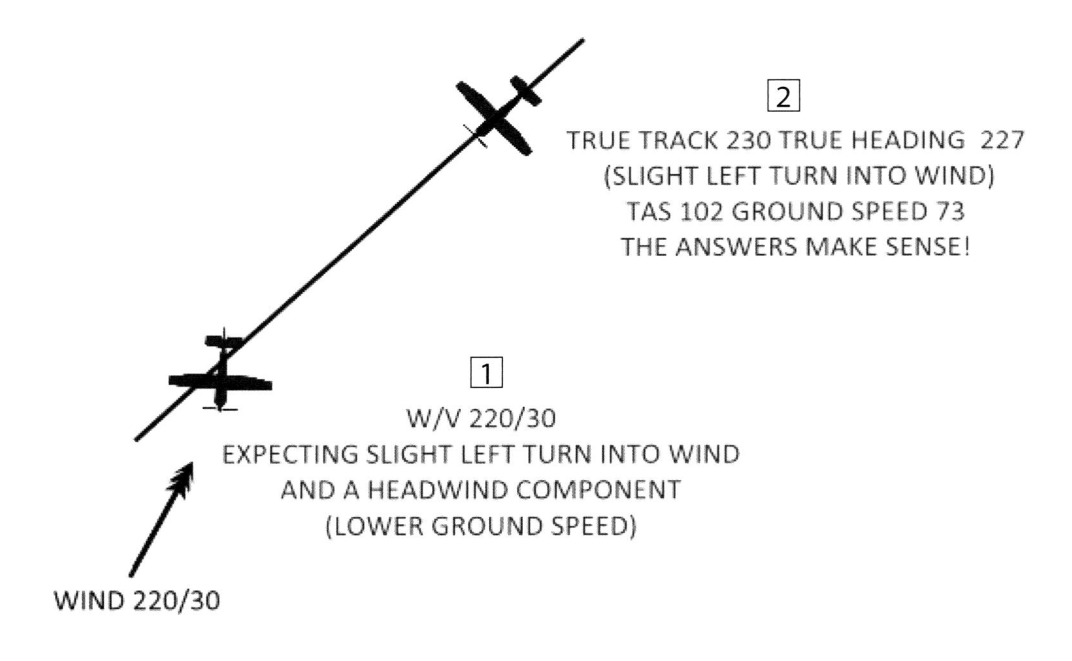

Lastly, we are asked to find the time it will take to fly the leg:

OUTER SCALE:	DISTANCE	SPEED
INNER SCALE:	TIME	▲ 60

Again, it is useful to have an idea of the answer we are expecting to get so that we can be confident that we have read the computer correctly. Very roughly a ground speed of 73 knots is close to 60, which would give us a rate over the ground of just under 1 nm per minute. The distance, 42 nm, divided by 1 gives an answer of 42, so we are anticipating an answer just under 40 minutes.

Back to the CRP, set the "60" mark on the rotating inner scale under the ground speed, here 73 knots. Re-set the moving lubber line to 42 nm (the distance) on the outer scale – here it helps to remember from school "speed = distance over time" i.e. distance is set on the outer scale OVER time on the inner.

Read off the time on the top of the inner scale 34.5 minutes.

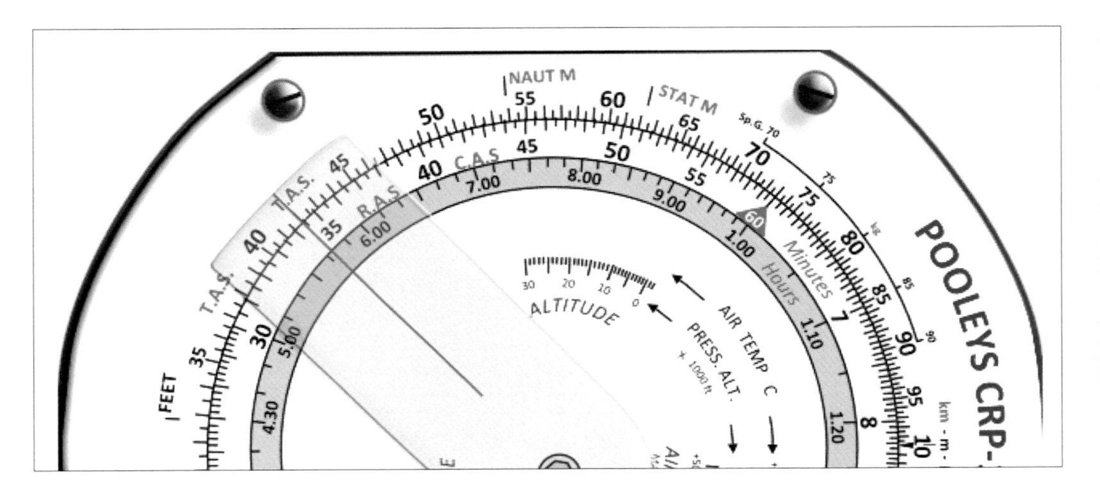

FURTHER READING: APM VOLUME 3, SECTION 2, CHAPTER 9– DRIFT

17. (Answer: D) 290/40.

1. Place centre dot on TAS, 110 knots
2. Set Heading, 260, under the index
3. The difference between heading and track is 15°. It is port drift as the track is to the left of the heading

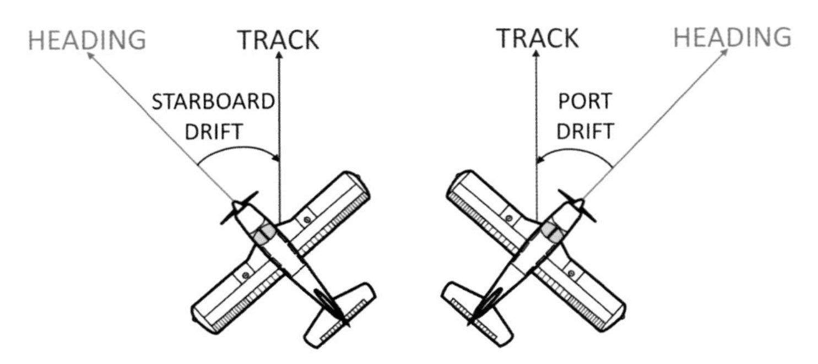

4. Follow the arc representing the groundspeed, 78 knots, and make a mark to represent the drift - 15° left
5. Now, move the centre dot down to the wind component grid.
6. Rotate the inner disc until your wind mark is below the centre dot.
7. Read off the wind direction under the index, 290 degrees and the velocity under the mark on the wind component grid, here 40 knots.

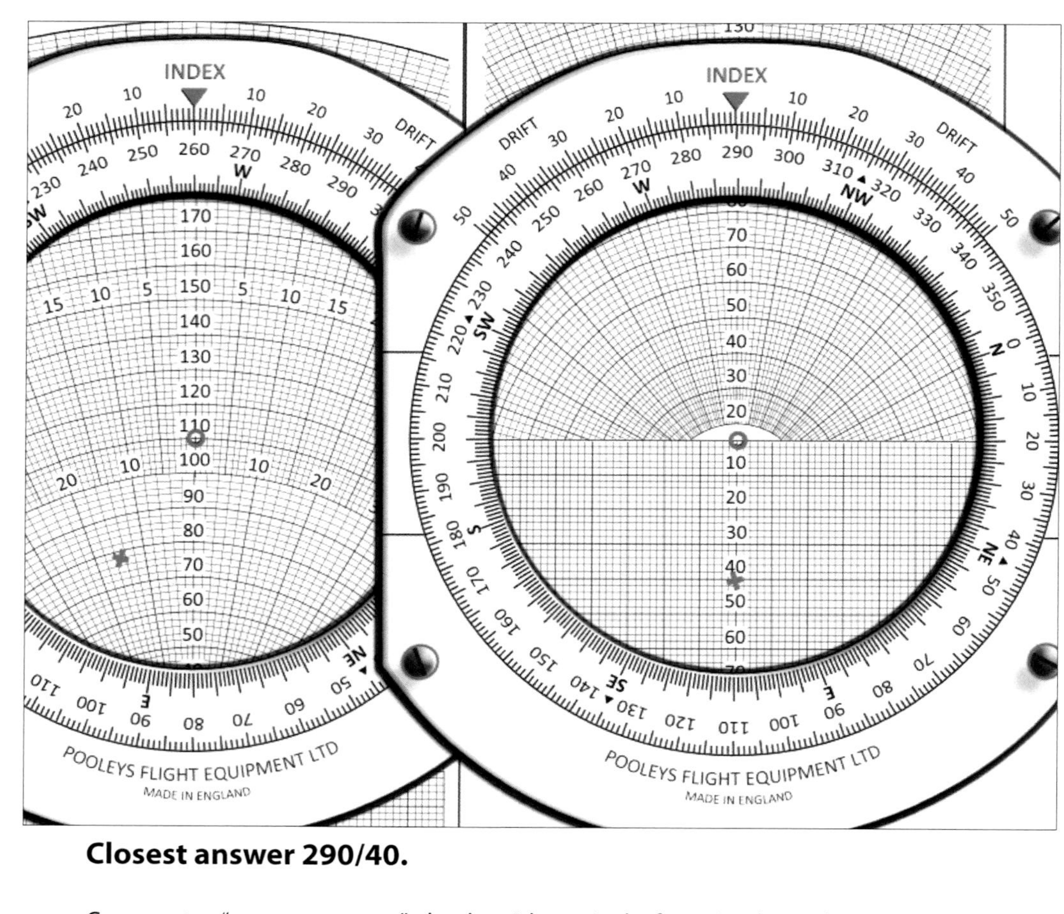

Closest answer 290/40.

Carry out a "common sense" check, with a wind of 290/40 kt and a track of 245, you would expect to turn right into wind (heading 260 achieves this), and we would expect an decrease in groundspeed due to a headwind. The answer we obtained therefore seems sensible.

FURTHER READING: APM VOLUME 3, SECTION 2, CHAPTER 9– DRIFT

18. (Answer: B) 0916 UTC.

To begin with find the ground speed:

1. Set the wind direction (150) on the rotating inner scale under the Index on the fixed outer scale.
2. Set the centre circle on a convenient speed arc – 100 is a handy round number. Mark down the wind speed, 40 knots for this question.
3. Move the sliding scale so that the centre circle is over the TAS 110.
4. Rotate the inner scale so that the measured true track, 180, is now below the index.
5. Read off the ground speed: 78 kt.

Carry out a common sense check: The difference between the heading 180 and the wind direction 150 is 30°; we can see that it is a headwind and can anticipate a groundspeed lower than the TAS.

40 x 0.9 = 36 knots
121 – 36 = 85 knots ground speed

OUTER SCALE:	DISTANCE	SPEED
INNER SCALE:	TIME	60

Rule of Thumb:

The cross wind component can be roughly calculated using the sine of number of degrees between the heading (or runway direction) and the wind direction. Similarly the cosine of that angle can be used to find a head or tailwind component.

SINE	CROSSWIND COMPONENT
30° = 0.5	50% of wind speed
40° = 0.6	60% of wind speed
50° = 0.7	70% of wind speed
60° = 0.9	90% of wind speed

COSINE	HEAD/TAIL WIND COMPONENT
30° = 0.9	90% of wind speed
40° = 0.75	75% of wind speed
50° = 0.6	60% of wind speed
60° = 0.5	50% of wind speed

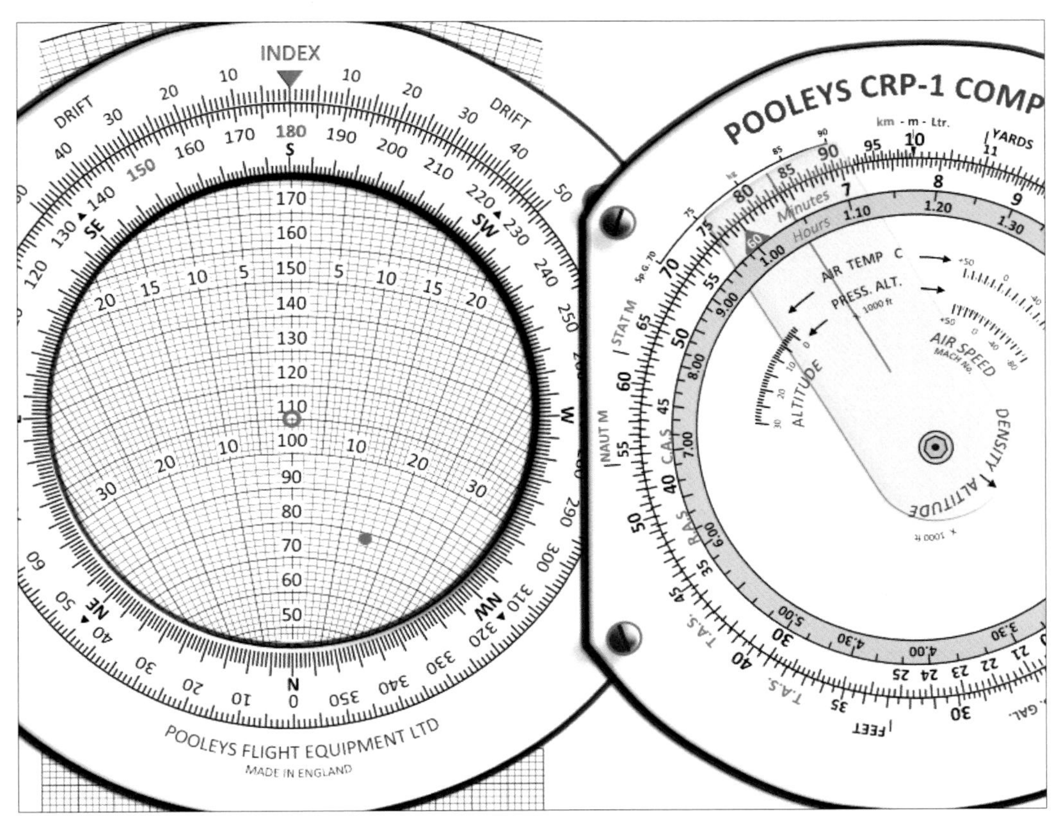

To find the time to point B:

1. Place the ground speed, 78 kt, over the time index.
2. On the outer scale find the distance 83 nm.
3. Read off the time on the inner scale: 64 minutes.
4. Again a common sense check shows that we expect an answer greater than 55 minutes. If we are travelling at nearly 1.5 nm per minute (90 kts): 83 ÷ 1.5 = 55 minutes.

Finally, add your result to the time to find the ETA: 0812 + 64 = 0916 UTC

FURTHER READING: APM VOLUME 3, SECTION 2, CHAPTER 9– DRIFT

19. (Answer: D) A rhumb line is a line which crosses all meridians of longitude at the same angle.

- A straight line drawn on a Transverse Mercator projection is a rhumb line.
- All parallels of latitude are rhumb lines, since they intersect with the meridians at the same angle.
- As a constant angle is maintained a rhumb line is easier to fly.

FURTHER READING: APM VOLUME 3, SECTION 1, CHAPTER 2 – AERONAUTICAL CHARTS

END OF EXPLANATIONS PAPER 4

INTENTIONALLY BLANK

EASA PPL REVISION PAPERS

INTENTIONALLY BLANK

PRACTICE PLANNING AND PLOGS

The following routes are provided to give practice in the practical application of the navigation planning techniques that you have learned and will put to use when cross country flying. **This section does not form part of the theoretical examination preparation, you will not be required to plot and plan a whole route. It is included to help you hone your navigation planning skills.**

NAVIGATION ROUTE 1

You are planning the following VFR flight:
From: Leicester (52 36 28N 001 01 55W)
To: Thruxton (51 12 38N 001 36 00W)
Via: Westcott NDB (WCO 51 51 18N 000 57 75W)
Alternate: Popham (51 11 63N 001 14 08W)

TAKE OFF:

LAND:

FLIGHT TIME:

FROM	TO	ALT/FL	SAFE ALT	TAS	W/V	TRK T	DRIFT	HDG T	VAR	HDG M	GS	DIST	TIME	ETA
LEICESTER 52 36 28N 001 01 55W	**WCO** 51 51 18N 000 57 75W	As Reqd.	1300	110	150/25				3W					
WCO 51 51 18N 000 57 75W	**THRUXTON** 51 12 38N 001 36 00W	As Reqd.	1300	110	150/25				3W					
										TOTAL				
ALTERNATE														
THRUXTON 51 12 38N 001 36 00W	**POPHAM** 51 11 63N 001 14 08W	As Reqd.	1300	110	160/20				3W					

Note: Safety Altitude is calculated from the higher of: i) the highest ground plus 1,299 feet; or ii) the highest structure plus 1,000 feet, within 5 nm of track rounded up to the next 100 feet

ANSWER: Completed Plog.

TAKE OFF:

LAND:

FLIGHT TIME:

FROM	TO	ALT/FL	SAFE ALT	TAS	W/V	TRK T	DRIFT	HDG T	VAR	HDG M	GS	DIST	TIME	ETA
LEICESTER 52 36 28N 001 01 55W	**WCO** 51 51 18N 000 57 75W	As Reqd.	2300	110	150/25	178	6S	172	3W	175	87	45	31	
WCO 51 51 18N 000 57 75W	**THRUXTON** 51 12 38N 001 36 00W	As Reqd.	2300	110	150/25	213	12S	201	3W	204	96	45	28	
										TOTAL		90	59	
ALTERNATE														
THRUXTON 51 12 38N 001 36 00W	**POPHAM** 51 11 63N 001 14 08W	As Reqd.	1800	110	160/20	095	10P	105	3W	108	100	13.7	8	

Note: Safety Altitude is calculated from the higher of: i) the highest ground plus 1,299 feet; or ii) the highest structure plus 1,000 feet, within 5 nm of track rounded up to the next 100 feet

Method: Legs Leicester to WCO; WCO to Thruxton:

1. Place the centre of the protractor over the track drawn on the map near the mid-point between the two ends of the track.
2. Align the grid marks on the protractor with the vertical meridian lines on the chart. Read off the True Track, in this case 178° for the first leg and 213 from WCO to Thuxton.
3. Next, find the effect of the wind on the aircraft. The wind vector is the same for both legs,so using your CRP computer set the wind direction (150) on the rotating inner scale under the Index on the fixed outer scale.
4. Set the centre circle on a convenient speed arc – 100 is a handy round number. Mark down the wind speed, 25 knots for this question.
5. Move the sliding scale so that the centre circle is over the TAS 110.

Leicester to WCO:

6. Rotate the inner scale so that the measured true track, 178, is now below the index. Note the wind mark is now displaced 8° to the right.
7. Rotate the inner scale 8° to the right, 178 is now below 8° on the right hand side of the fixed drift scale. However, now the pencil mark indicates 6° of starboard drift. What we are aiming for is parity, so move the rotating scale so that 178 is below 6° on the fixed drift scale and still right of the index. In so doing the drift remains at 6° and we have parity – the track is offset 6° and the wind mark still shows 6°.

8. Read off the true heading under the Index = 172°.

9. Finally apply the variation, in this case 3°W. Remember "East is Least, West is Best", the variation is West, hence we add it giving a magnetic heading of 175°.

10. Read the ground speed under the wind dot – 87 knots.

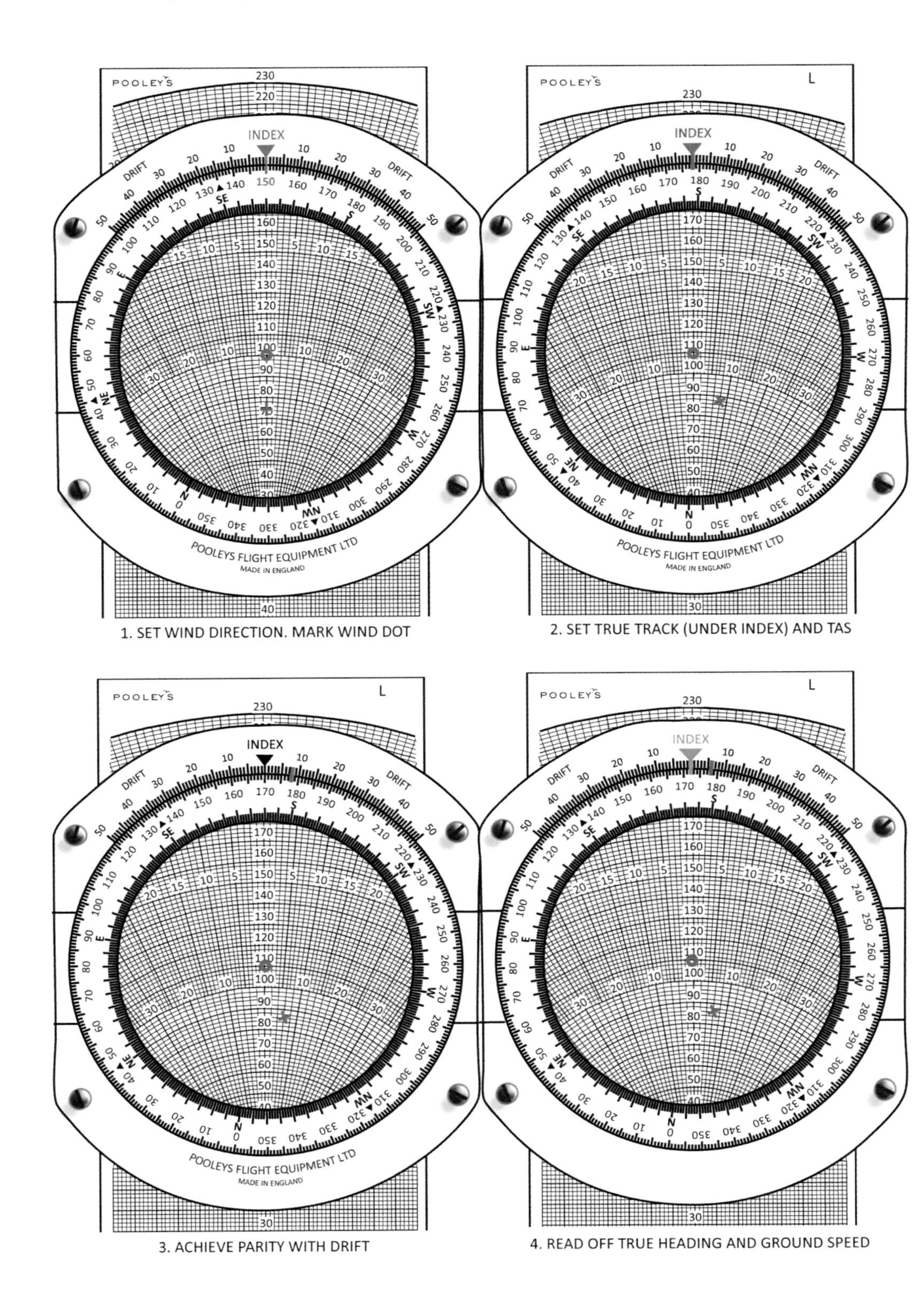

1. SET WIND DIRECTION. MARK WIND DOT

2. SET TRUE TRACK (UNDER INDEX) AND TAS

3. ACHIEVE PARITY WITH DRIFT

4. READ OFF TRUE HEADING AND GROUND SPEED

WCO to Thruxton:

As the wind is the same for the second leg, rotate the inner scale so that the measured true track, 213, is now below the index. You can repeat stages 6 to 10 above.

Following the same method as before we find a true heading of 201 to which we add the variation of 3°W to obtain the magnetic heading of 204. The groundspeed is 96 knots for this leg.

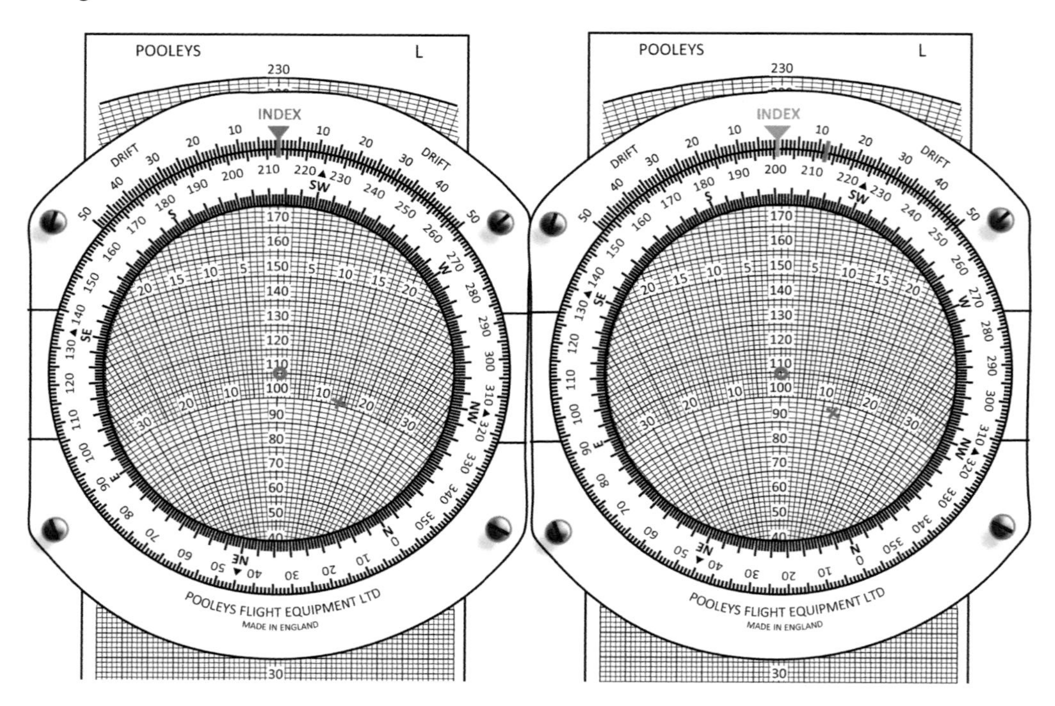

The CRP can be very easy to misread, drawing a small sketch of the route will give you a rough idea of the answers you expect to obtain and ensure that any amendments are applied correctly.

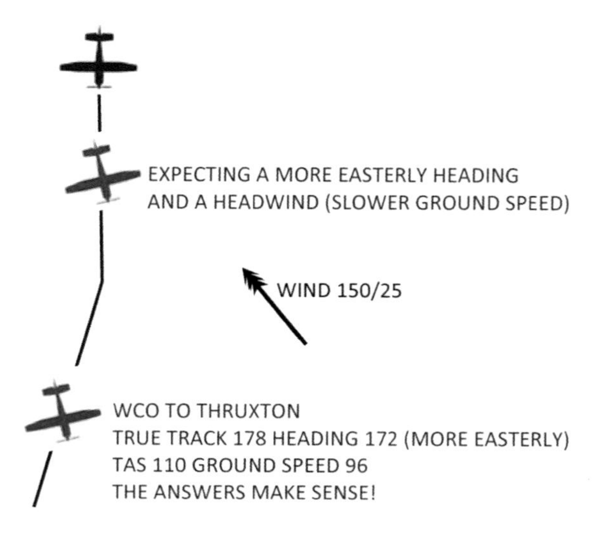

Diversion leg: Thruxton to Popham

NOTE: THAT FOR THIS LEG A DIFFERENT FORECAST WIND IS USED.

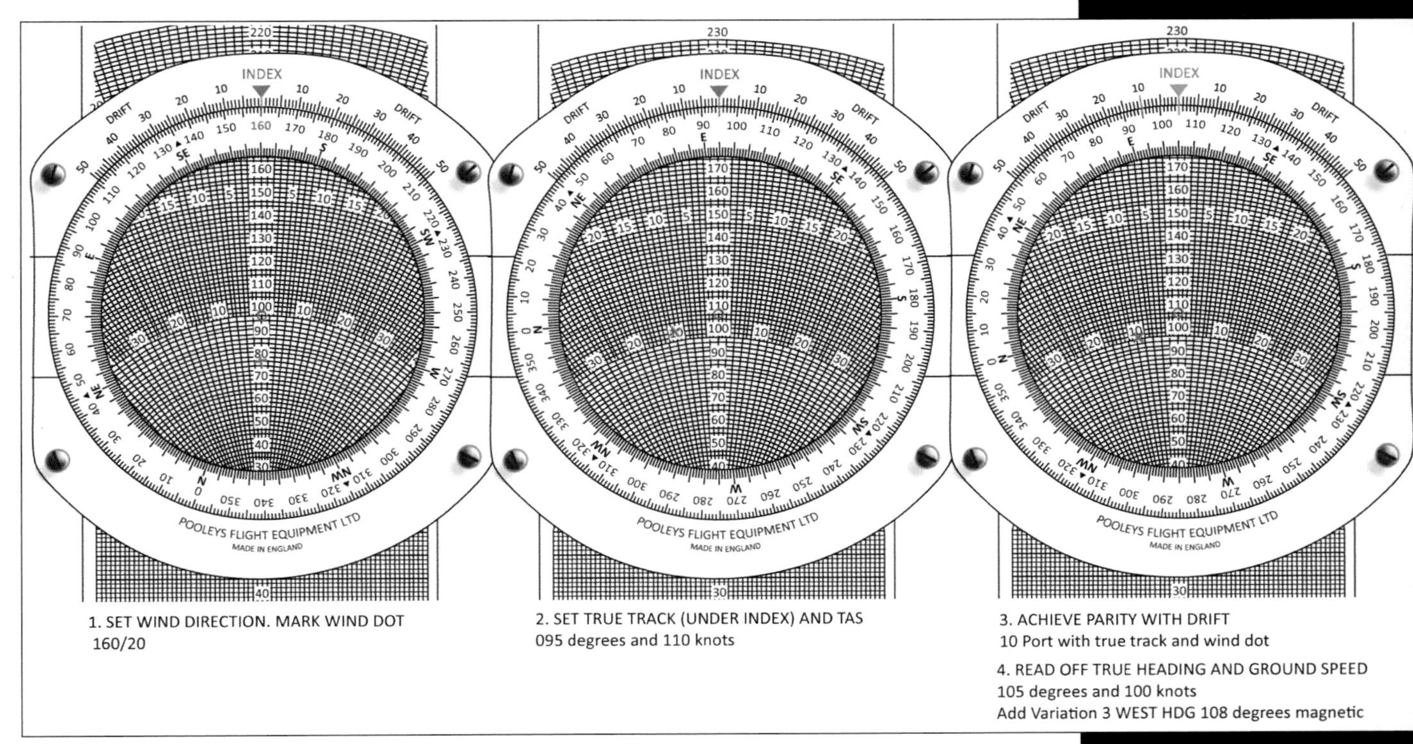

1. SET WIND DIRECTION. MARK WIND DOT 160/20

2. SET TRUE TRACK (UNDER INDEX) AND TAS 095 degrees and 110 knots

3. ACHIEVE PARITY WITH DRIFT 10 Port with true track and wind dot

4. READ OFF TRUE HEADING AND GROUND SPEED 105 degrees and 100 knots Add Variation 3 WEST HDG 108 degrees magnetic

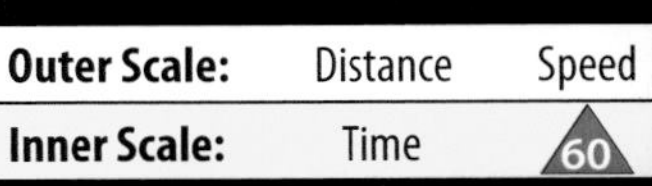

Outer Scale:	Distance	Speed
Inner Scale:	Time	60

To complete the plog calculations, use the front of the CRP to determine the time for each leg.

1. Set the calculated ground speed above the time index.
2. Find the distance for each leg on the outer scale.
3. Read off the time on the inner scale.

The CRP illustrated below is set for the second leg from WCO to Thruxton.

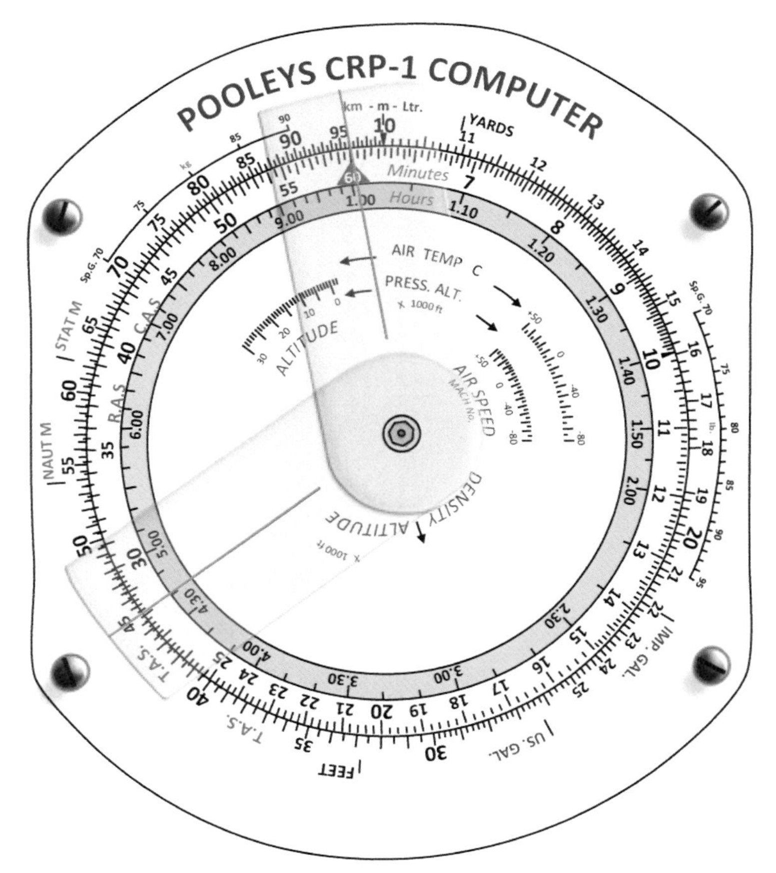

NAVIGATION ROUTE 2

You are planning the following VFR flight:
From: Caernarfon (53 06 27N 004 20 42W)
To: Exeter (50 44 05N 003 24 84W)
Via: Aberystwyth (52 25 02N 004 05 00W)
and Swansea aerodrome (51 36 04N 004 04 20W)
Alternate: Dunkeswell (50 51 60N 003 14 08W)

TAKE OFF:

LAND:

FLIGHT TIME:

FROM	TO	ALT/FL	SAFE ALT	TAS	W/V	TRK T	DRIFT	HDG T	VAR	HDG M	GS	DIST	TIME	ETA
CAERNAFON 53 06 27N 004 20 42W	**ABERYSTWYTH** 52 25 02N 004 05 00W	As req.	4300	110	230/30				3.5W					
ABERYSTWYTH 52 25 02N 004 05 00W	**SWANSEA** 51 36 04N 004 04 20W	As req.	4300	110	230/30				3.5W					
SWANSEA 51 36 04N 004 04 20W	**EXETER** 50 44 05N 003 24 84W	As req.	3500	110	230/30				3W					
										TOTAL				
ALTERNATE														
EXETER 50 44 05N 003 24 84W	**DUNKESWELL** 50 51 60N 003 14 08W	As req.	2200	110	250/20				3W					

Note: Safety Altitude is calculated from the higher of: i) the highest ground plus 1,299 feet; or ii) the highest structure plus 1,000 feet, within 5 nm of track rounded up to the next 100 feet

ANSWER: Completed Plog.

TAKE OFF:

LAND:

FLIGHT TIME:

FROM	TO	ALT/FL	SAFE ALT	TAS	W/V	TRK T	DRIFT	HDG T	VAR	HDG M	GS	DIST	TIME	ETA
CAERNARFON 53 06 27N 004 20 42W	**ABERYSTWYTH** 52 25 02N 004 05 00W	As req.	4900	110	230/30	168	14 P	182	3W	185	93	42.3	27.2	
ABERYSTWYTH 52 25 02N 004 05 00W	**SWANSEA** 51 36 04N 004 04 20W	As req.	4900	110	230/30	180	11 P	191	3W	194	89	49.0	33	
SWANSEA 51 36 04N 004 04 20W	**EXETER** 50 44 05N 003 24 84W	As req.	3500	110	230/30	156	15 P	171	3W	174	99	57.6	34.9	
										TOTAL		148.9	95.1	
ALTERNATE														
EXETER 50 44 05N 003 24 84W	**DUNKESWELL** 50 51 60N 003 14 08W	As req.	2200	110	250/20	043	5 S	038	3W	041	128	10.2	4.8	

Note: Safety Altitude is calculated from the higher of: i) the highest ground plus 1,299 feet; or ii) the highest structure plus 1,000 feet, within 5 nm of track rounded up to the next 100 feet

Method: Caernafon to Aberystwyth; Aberystwyth to Swansea; Swansea to Exeter

1. Place the centre of the protractor over the track drawn on the map near the mid-point between the two ends of the track.
2. Align the grid marks on the protractor with the vertical meridian lines on the chart. Read off the True Track, in this case 168°, 180° and 156°.
3. Next we need to find the effect of the wind on the aircraft. The same wind vector is forecast for all three legs, using your CRP computer set the wind direction (230) on the rotating inner scale under the Index on the fixed outer scale.
4. Set the centre circle on a convenient speed arc – 100 is a handy round number. Mark down the wind speed, 30 knots for this question.
5. Move the sliding scale so that the centre circle is over the TAS 110.

Leg One: Caernafon to Aberystwyth

6. Rotate the inner scale so that the measured true track, 168, is now below the index. Note the wind mark that was drawn is now displaced 15° to the left.

7. Now rotate the inner scale 15° to the left, 168 is now below 15° on the left hand side of the fixed drift scale. However, now the pencil mark indicates 14° of port drift. What we are aiming for is parity, so move the rotating scale so that 168 is below 14° on the fixed drift scale and still left of the index. In so doing the drift remains at 14° and we have parity – the track is offset 14° and the wind mark still shows 14°.

8. Read off the true heading under the Index = 182°.

9. Finally, on your plog apply the variation, in this case 3°W. Remember "East is Least, West is Best", the variation is West, hence we add it giving a magnetic heading of 185°.

10. Read the ground speed under the wind dot – 93 knots.

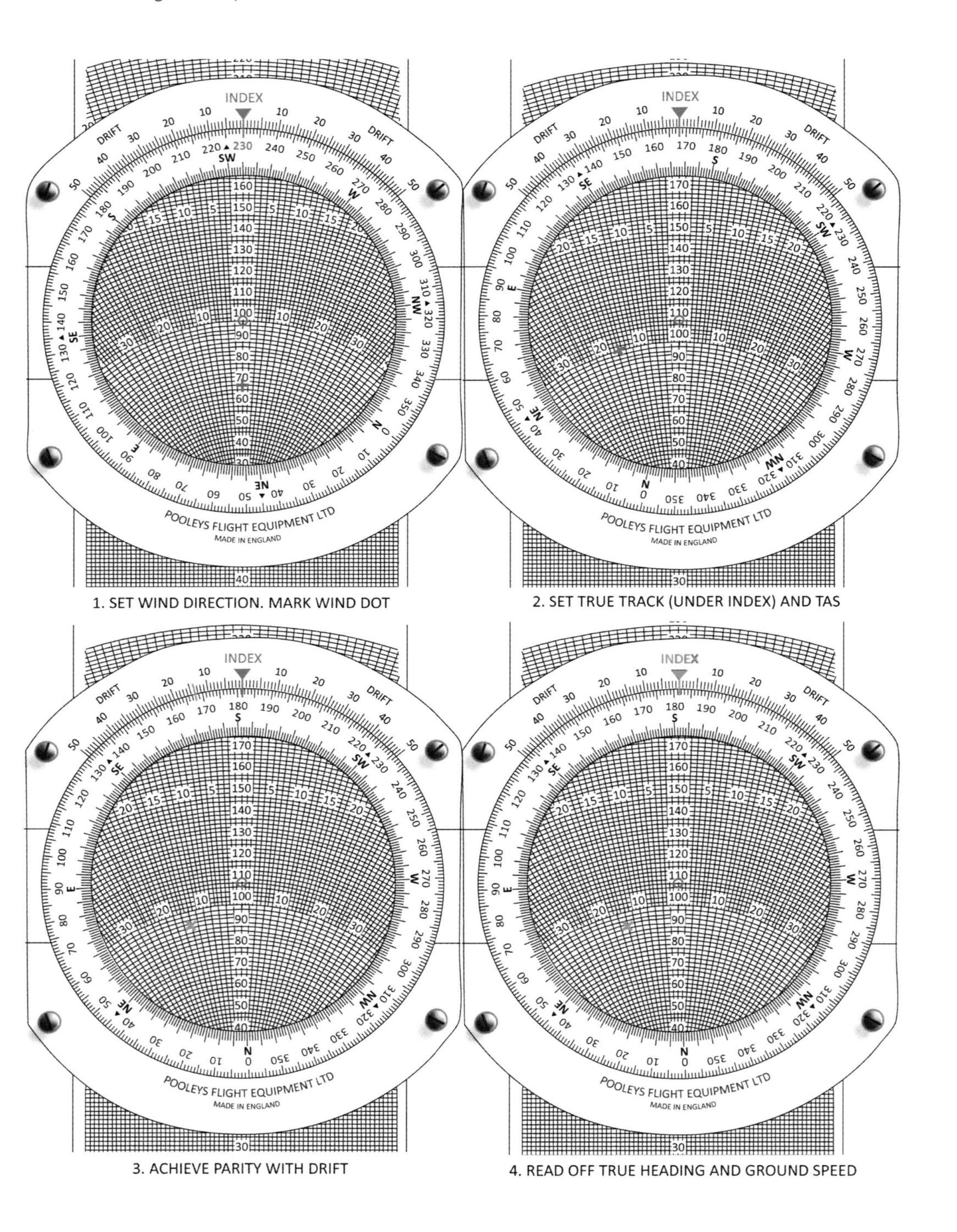

1. SET WIND DIRECTION. MARK WIND DOT

2. SET TRUE TRACK (UNDER INDEX) AND TAS

3. ACHIEVE PARITY WITH DRIFT

4. READ OFF TRUE HEADING AND GROUND SPEED

Leg Two: Aberystwyth to Swansea

As the wind is the same for the second leg, rotate the inner scale so that the measured true track, 180°, is now below the index. You can repeat stages 6 to 10 above.

Following the same method as before we find a true heading of 191° to which we add the variation of 3°W to obtain the magnetic heading of 194°. The groundspeed is 89 knots for this leg.

Leg Three: Swansea to Exeter

As the wind is the same for the second leg, rotate the inner scale so that the measured true track, 156°, is now below the index. You can repeat stages 6 to 10 above.

Following the same method as before we find a true heading of 171° to which we add the variation of 3°W to obtain the magnetic heading of 174°. The groundspeed is 99 knots for this leg.

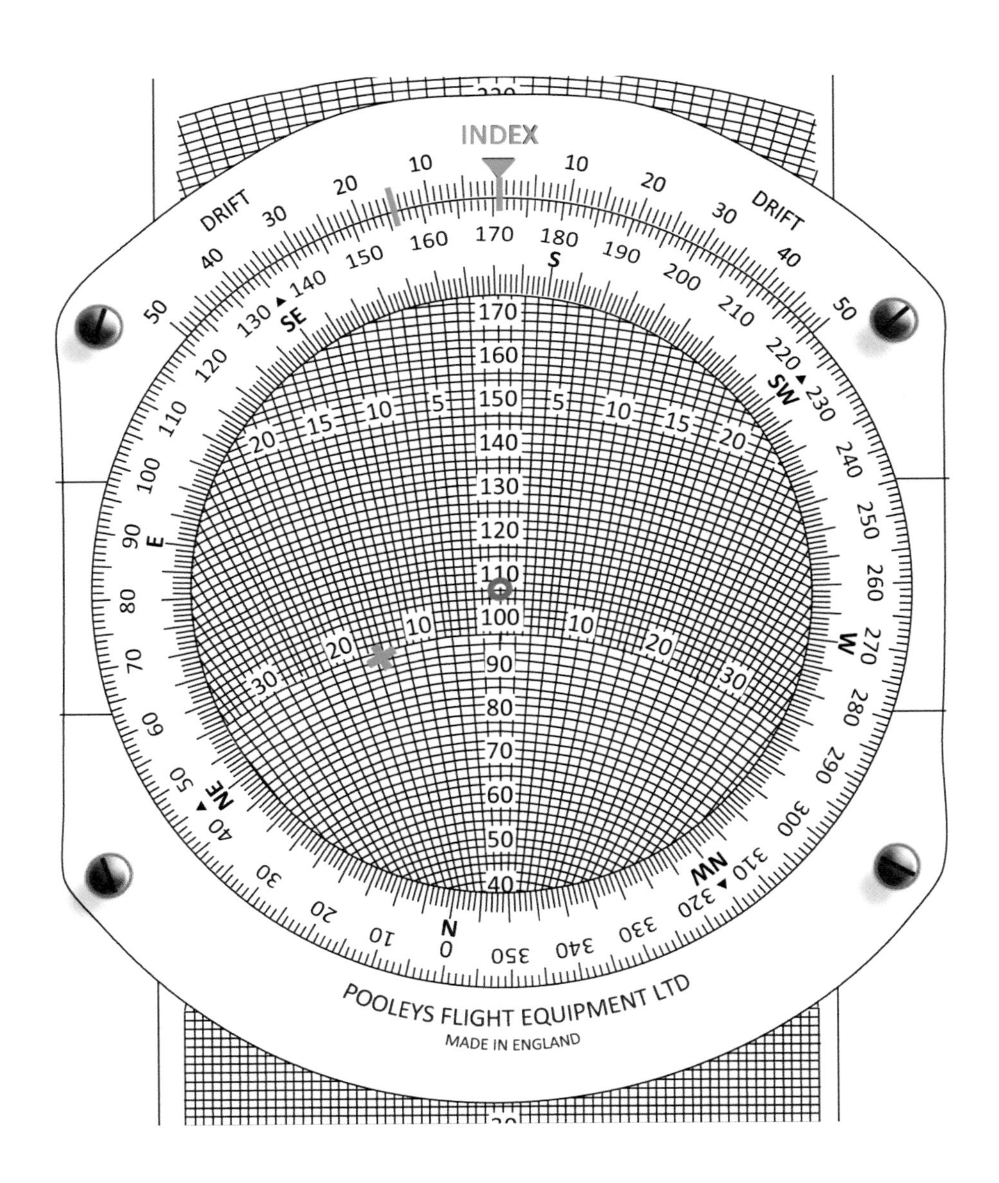

The CRP can be very easy to misread, when using it drawing a small sketch of the route is a good way to get a rough idea of the answer you expect to obtain and to ensure that any amendments are applied correctly.

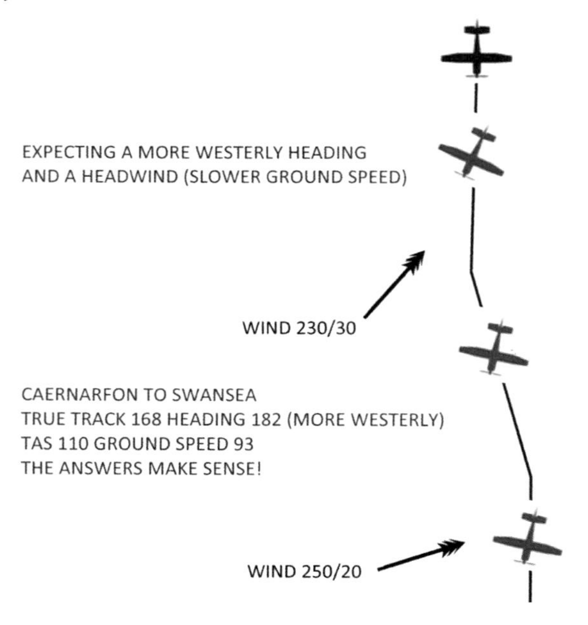

Diversion: Exeter to Dunkeswell

A different wind vector is forecast for this leg and so this will need to be changed on the CRP for this leg:

1. Set the new wind direction (250) on the rotating inner scale under the Index on the fixed outer scale.

2. Set the centre circle on a convenient speed arc – 100 is a handy round number. Mark down the wind speed, 20 knots for this question.

3. Move the sliding scale so that the centre circle is over the TAS 110.

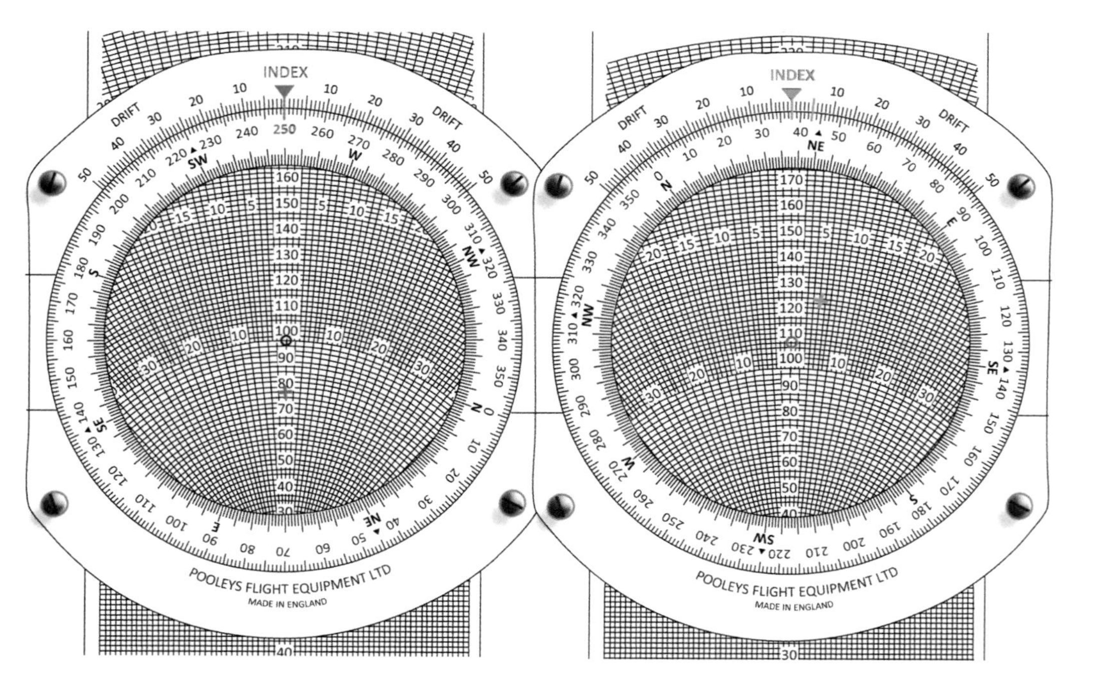

To complete the plog calculations, use the front of the CRP to determine the time for each leg.

1. Set the calculated ground speed above the time index.
2. Find the distance for each leg on the outer scale.
3. Read off the time on the inner scale.

Outer Scale:	Distance	Speed
Inner Scale:	Time	60

NAVIGATION ROUTE 3

You are planning the following VFR flight:
From: Bodmin (50 30 06N 004 39 96W)
To: Wycombe (51 36 70N 000 48 49W)
Via: Melksham (51 22 45N 002 08 30W)
Alternate: Blackbushe (51 19 42N 000 50 90W)

TAKE OFF:

LAND:

FLIGHT TIME:

FROM	TO	ALT/FL	SAFE ALT	TAS	W/V	TRK T	DRIFT	HDG T	VAR	HDG M	GS	DIST	TIME	ETA
BODMIN 50 30 06N 004 39 96W	**MELKSHAM** 51 22 45N 002 08 30W	As req.	2800	100	330/35				3W					
MELKSHAM 51 22 45N 002 08 30W	**WYCOMBE** 51 36 70N 000 48 49 W	As req.	3300	100	320/25				2W					
										TOTAL				
ALTERNATE														
WYCOMBE 51 36 70N 000 48 49W	**BLACKBUSHE** 51 19 42N 000 50 90W	As req.	1300	100	320/25				2W					

Note: Safety Altitude is calculated from the higher of: i) the highest ground plus 1,299 feet; or ii) the highest structure plus 1,000 feet, within 5 nm of track rounded up to the next 100 feet

ANSWER: Completed Plog.

TAKE OFF:

LAND:

FLIGHT TIME:

FROM	TO	ALT/FL	SAFE ALT	TAS	W/V	TRK T	DRIFT	HDG T	VAR	HDG M	GS	DIST	TIME	ETA
BODMIN 50 30 06N 004 39 96W	**MELKSHAM** 51 22 45N 002 08 30W	As req.	2800	100	330/35	061	20 S	041	3W	044	95	109	69	
MELKSHAM 51 22 45N 002 08 30W	**WYCOMBE** 51 36 70N 000 48 49 W	As req.	3300	100	320/25	074	13 S	061	2W	063	107	51.7	29	
										TOTAL		160.7	98	
ALTERNATE														
WYCOMBE 51 36 70N 000 48 49W	**BLACKBUSHE** 51 19 42N 000 50 90W	As req.	1300	100	320/25	185	10 P	195	2W	197	116	17.3	9.1	

Note: Safety Altitude is calculated from the higher of: i) the highest ground plus 1,299 feet; or ii) the highest structure plus 1,000 feet, within 5 nm of track rounded up to the next 100 feet

METHOD:

1. Place the centre of the protractor over the track drawn on the map near the mid-point between the two ends of the track.
2. Align the grid marks on the protractor with the graticule lines on the chart. Read off the True Track, in this case 061°. 074° and 185°.

FIRST LEG: Bodmin to Melksham;

3. Next, find the effect of the wind on the aircraft. Using the CRP computer set the wind direction (330°) on the rotating inner scale under the Index on the fixed outer scale.

4. Set the centre circle on a convenient speed arc – 100 is a handy round number. Mark down the wind speed, 35 knots for this route.

5. The TAS is 100, so the centre circle is already in the correct place.

6. Rotate the inner scale so that the measured true track, 061°, is now below the index. Note the wind mark is now displaced 20° to the right

7. Rotate the inner scale 20° to the right, 061° is now below 20° on the right hand side of the fixed drift scale. We are aiming for parity, so ensure that the wind dot is still displaced 20°.

8. Read off the true heading under the Index = 041°

9. Finally apply the variation, in this case 3°W. Remember "East is Least, West is Best", the variation is West, hence we add it giving a magnetic heading of 044°

10. Read off the groundspeed below the wind dot – 95 knots.

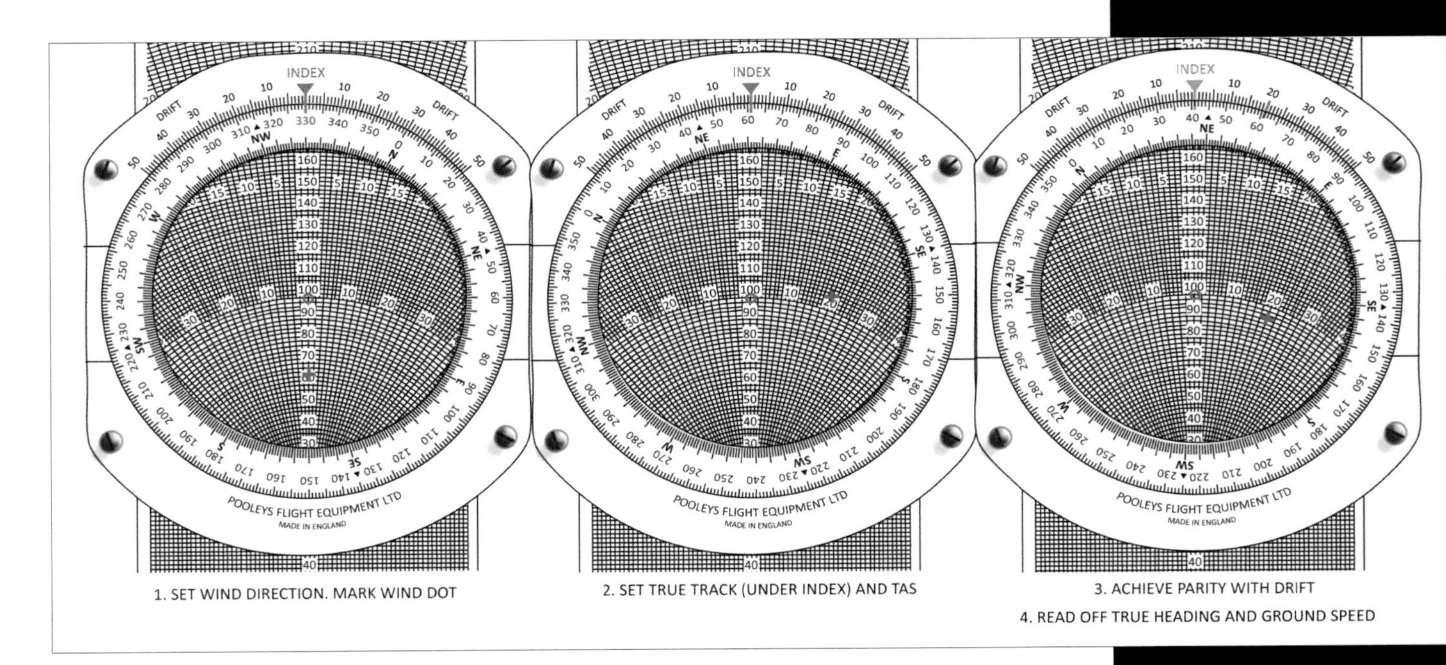

1. SET WIND DIRECTION. MARK WIND DOT

2. SET TRUE TRACK (UNDER INDEX) AND TAS

3. ACHIEVE PARITY WITH DRIFT

4. READ OFF TRUE HEADING AND GROUND SPEED

SECOND LEG: Melksham to Wycombe

NOTE: A DIFFERENT FORECAST WIND IS USED AND WE MUST "RESET" THE CRP

3. Set the wind direction (320) on the rotating inner scale under the Index on the fixed outer scale.

4. Set the centre circle on a convenient speed arc – 100 is a handy round number. Mark down the wind speed, 25 knots for this route.

5. The TAS is 100, so the centre circle is already in the correct place.

6. Rotate the inner scale so that the measured true track, 074°, is now below the index. Note the wind mark is now displaced 14° to the right.

7. Rotate the inner scale 14° to the right, 074° is now below 14° on the right hand side of the fixed drift scale. We are aiming for parity, but the wind dot now indicates 13°, so move 074° under 13° on the fixed drift scale. Check that the wind dot is still displaced 13°.

8. Read off the true heading under the Index = 061°.

9. Finally apply the variation, in this case 2°W. Remember "East is Least, West is Best", the variation is West, hence we add it giving a magnetic heading of 063°.

10. Read off the groundspeed below the wind dot – 107 knots.

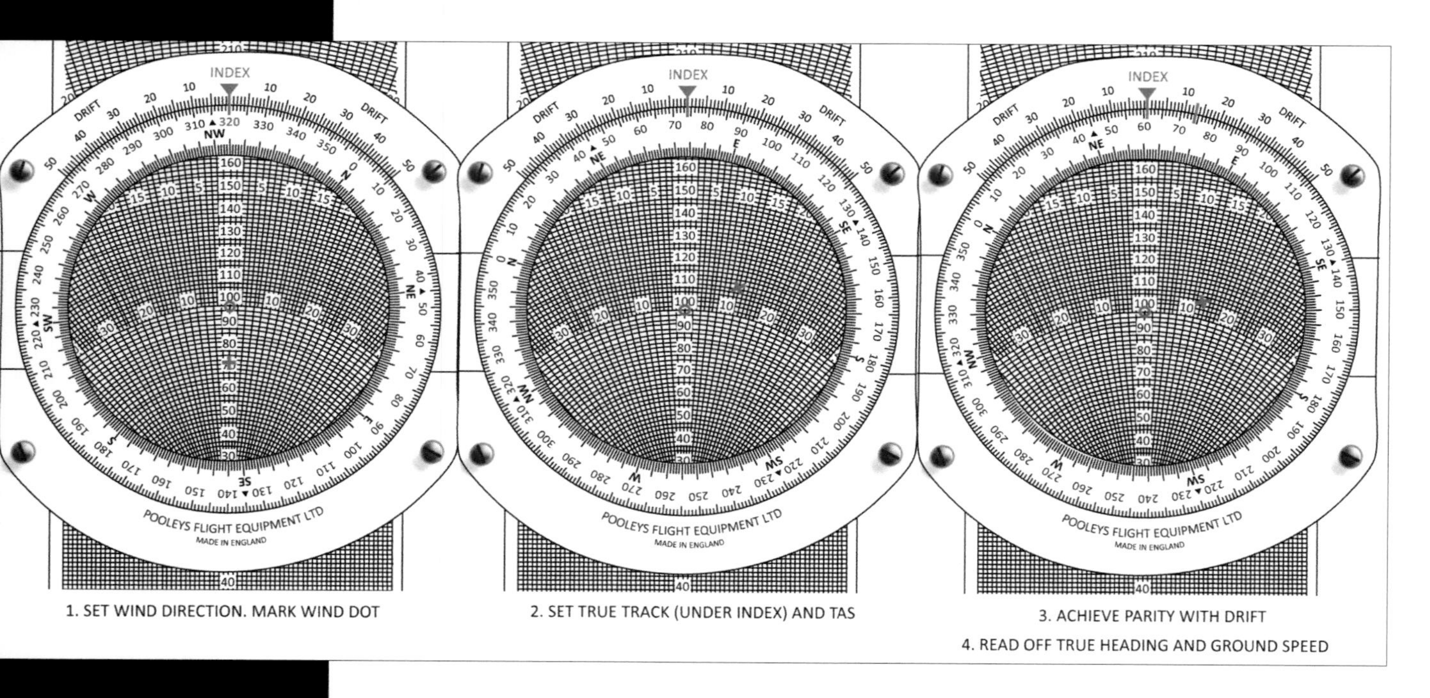

1. SET WIND DIRECTION. MARK WIND DOT

2. SET TRUE TRACK (UNDER INDEX) AND TAS

3. ACHIEVE PARITY WITH DRIFT

4. READ OFF TRUE HEADING AND GROUND SPEED

Diversion: Wycombe to Blackbushe

The diversion uses the same wind as leg two, so set the measured track of 185° below the index and repeat stages 6 to 10. This will give a magnetic heading of 197° and a ground speed of 116 knots.

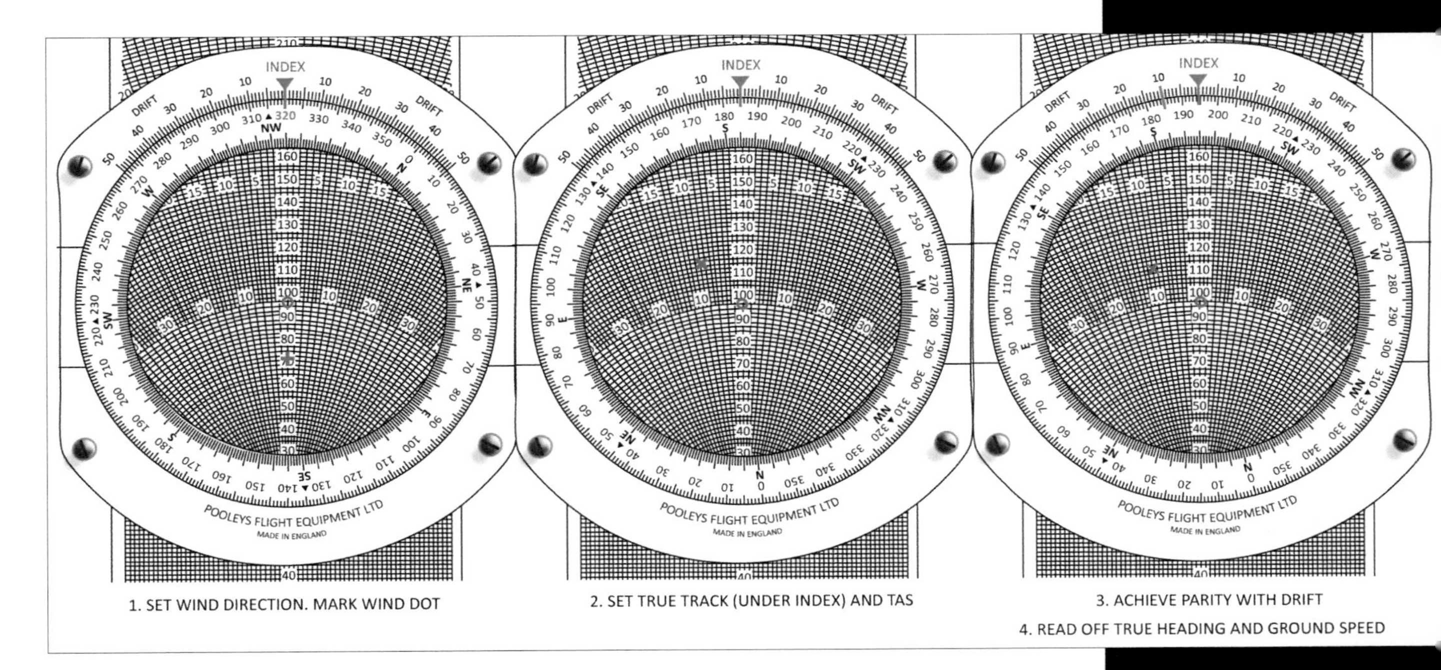

The CRP can be very easy to misread, making a small sketch will give you a rough idea of the answer you expect to obtain to ensure that any amendments are applied correctly.

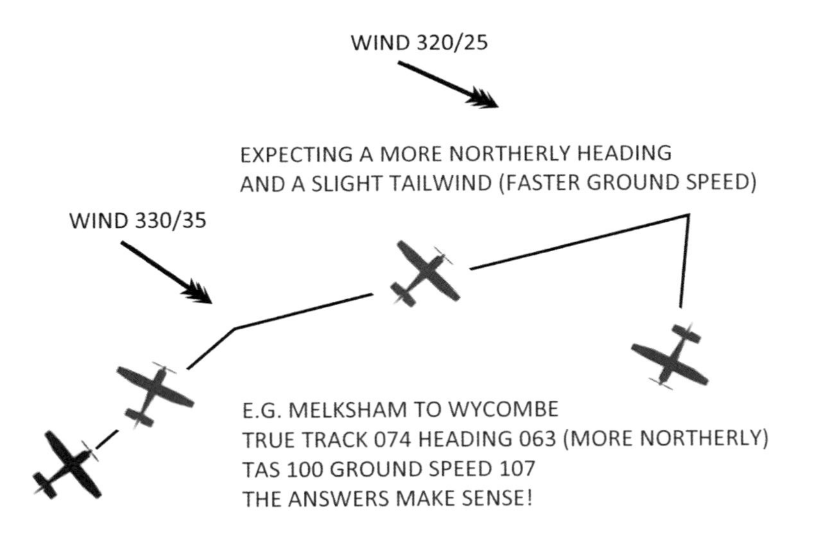

To complete the plog calculations, use the front of the CRP to determine the time for each leg.

1. Set the calculated ground speed above the time index.
2. Find the distance for each leg on the outer scale.
3. Read off the time on the inner scale.

NAVIGATION ROUTE 4

You are planning the following VFR flight:
From: Rochester (51 21 07N 000 30 30E)
To: Peterborough/Conington (52 27 90N000 15 28W)
Via: Elmsett (52 04 51N 000 58 65E)
Alternate: Bourn (52 12 88N 000 02 47W)

TAKE OFF:

LAND:

FLIGHT TIME:

FROM	TO	ALT/FL	SAFE ALT	TAS	W/V	TRK T	DRIFT	HDG T	VAR	HDG M	GS	DIST	TIME	ETA
ROCHESTER 51 21 17N 000 30 30E	**ELMSETT** 52 04 51N 000 58 65E	As req.	1900	95	040/20				2W					
ELMSETT 52 04 51N 000 58 65E	**CONINGTON** 52 27 90N 000 15 28W	As req.	1600	95	040/20				2W					
										TOTAL				
ALTERNATE														
CONINGTON 52 27 90N 000 15 28W	**BOURN** 52 12 88N 000 02 47W	As req.	1300	95	050/15				2W					

Note: Safety Altitude is calculated from the higher of: i) the highest ground plus 1,299 feet; or ii) the highest structure plus 1,000 feet, within 5 nm of track rounded up to the next 100 feet

ANSWER: Completed Plog.

TAKE OFF:

LAND:

FLIGHT TIME:

FROM	TO	ALT/FL	SAFE ALT	TAS	W/V	TRK T	DRIFT	HDG T	VAR	HDG M	GS	DIST	TIME	ETA
ROCHESTER 51 21 07N 000 30 10E	**ELMSETT** 52 04 51N 000 58 65E	As req.	1900	95	040/20	023	4 P	026	2W	028	75	46.8	37.4	
ELMSETT 52 04 51N 000 58 65E	**CONINGTON** 52 27 90N 000 15 28W	As req.	1600	95	040/20	298	12 P	310	2W	312	97	50.9	31.5	
										TOTAL		97.7	68.9	
ALTERNATE														
CONINGTON 52 27 90N 000 15 28W	**BOURN** 52 12 88N 000 02 47W	As req.	1300	95	050/15	154	9 S	145	2W	147	98	16.9	10.4	

Note: Safety Altitude is calculated from the higher of: i) the highest ground plus 1,299 feet; or ii) the highest structure plus 1,000 feet, within 5 nm of track rounded up to the next 100 feet

Method: Rochester to Elmsett; Elmsett to Conington

1. Place the centre of the protractor over the track drawn on the map near the mid-point between the two ends of the track.
2. Align the grid marks on the protractor with the graticule lines on the chart. Read off the True Track, in this case 023°, 298° and 154°.
3. Next, find the effect of the wind on the aircraft. Using the CRP computer set the wind direction for the first two legs (040) on the rotating inner scale under the Index on the fixed outer scale.
4. Set the centre circle on a convenient speed arc – 100 is a handy round number. Mark down the wind speed, 20 knots for this question.

Leg One: Rochester to Elmsett

5. Move the sliding scale so that the centre circle is over the TAS 95.
6. Rotate the inner scale so that the measured true track, 023°, is now below the index. Note the wind mark that was drawn is now displaced 5° to the left.

7. Now rotate the inner scale 5° to the left, 023° is now below 5° on the left hand side of the fixed drift scale. However, the wind dot is now only displaced by 4°; adjust the inner scale so that 023° is now under 4° on the fixed drift scale. Check to ensure that the wind dot is still displaced 4° to the left. We are aiming for parity, so if 023° is below 4° on the fixed drift scale and the wind dot is also displaced by 4° then the computer is set correctly.

8. Read off the true heading under the Index = 026°.

9. Finally apply the variation, in this case 2°W. Remember "East is Least, West is Best", the variation is West, hence we add it giving a magnetic heading of 028°.

10. Read the groundspeed below the wind dot – 75 knots.

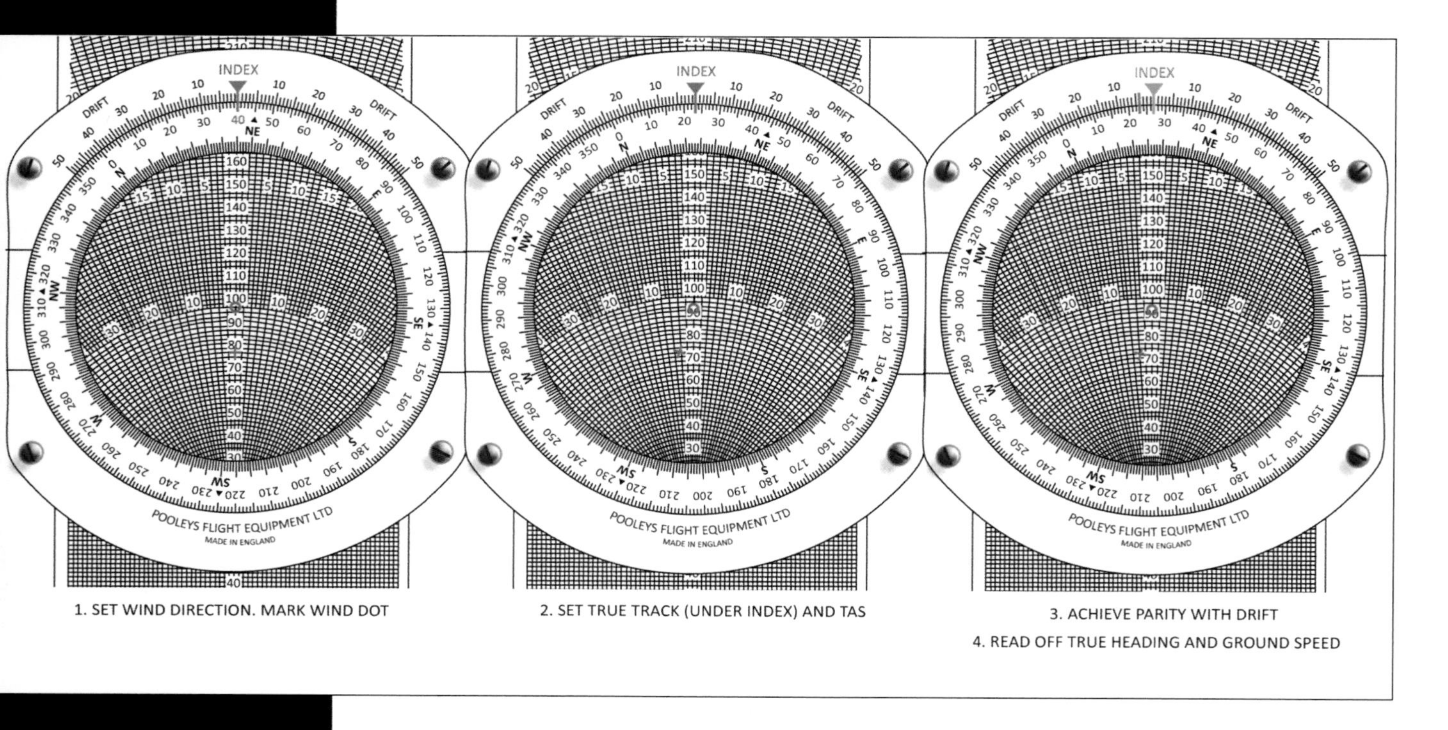

1. SET WIND DIRECTION. MARK WIND DOT

2. SET TRUE TRACK (UNDER INDEX) AND TAS

3. ACHIEVE PARITY WITH DRIFT

4. READ OFF TRUE HEADING AND GROUND SPEED

Leg Two: Elmsett to Conington

The wind vector for this leg is the same and so we can use the wind as set for the first leg.

1. Rotate the inner scale so that the measured true track, 298°, is now below the index.

2. Note the wind mark that was drawn is now displaced 12° to the left.

3. Rotate the inner scale 12° to the left, 298° is now below 12° on the left hand side of the fixed drift scale. The wind dot is still indicating 12° of port drift, so we have parity between the wind dot and the displacement of the true track.

4. Read off the true heading under the Index = 310°.

5. Finally apply the variation, in this case 2°W. Remember "East is Least, West is Best", the variation is West, hence we add it giving a magnetic heading of 312°.

6. Read the groundspeed below the wind dot – 97 knots.

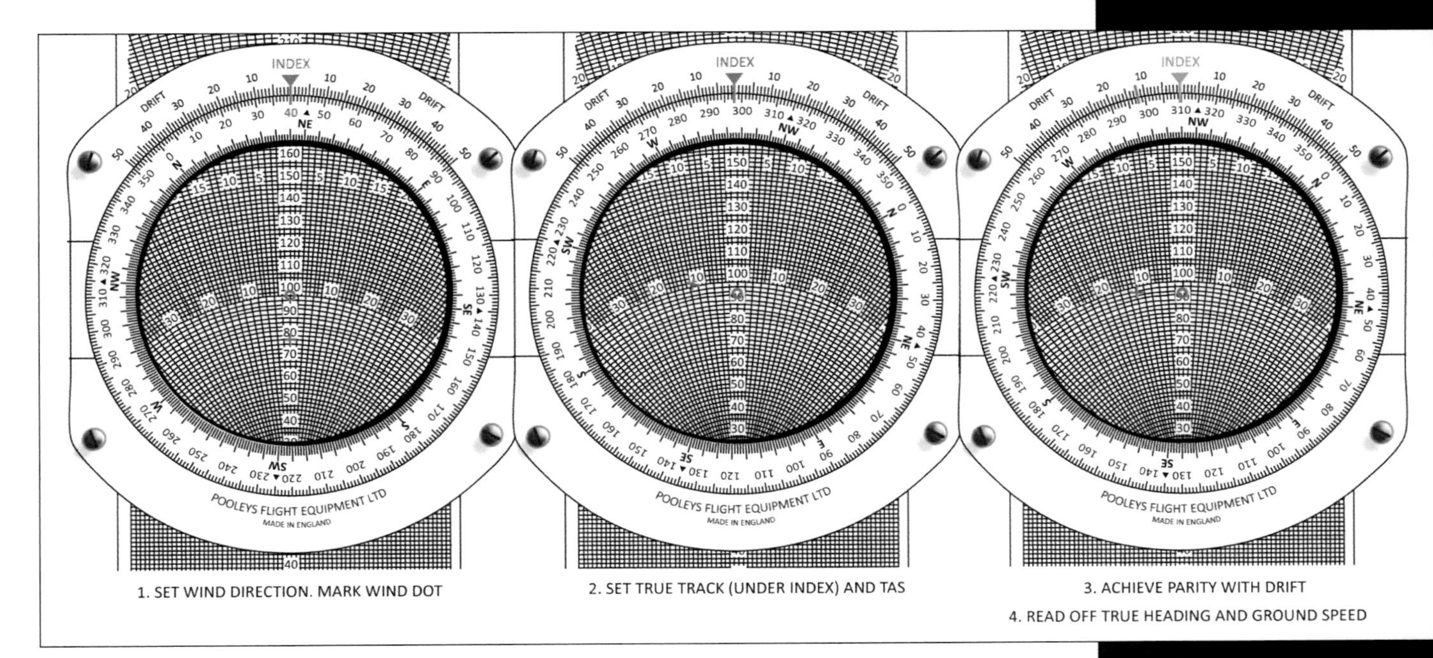

1. SET WIND DIRECTION. MARK WIND DOT

2. SET TRUE TRACK (UNDER INDEX) AND TAS

3. ACHIEVE PARITY WITH DRIFT

4. READ OFF TRUE HEADING AND GROUND SPEED

Diversion: Conington to Bourn

For this leg a new wind vector must be drawn.

1. To find the effect of the wind on the aircraft. Using the CRP computer set the wind direction (050°) on the rotating inner scale under the Index on the fixed outer scale.
2. Set the centre circle on a convenient speed arc – 100 is a handy round number. Mark down the wind speed, 15 knots for this question.
3. Move the sliding scale so that the centre circle is over the TAS 95.
4. Rotate the inner scale so that the measured true track, 154°, is below the index.

NOTE: THE WIND MARK THAT WAS DRAWN IS NOW DISPLACED 9° TO THE RIGHT.

5. Rotate the inner scale 9° to the right, 154° is now below 9° on the right hand side of the fixed drift scale. The wind dot is still indicating 9° of starboard drift, so we have parity between the wind dot and the displacement of the true track.
6. Read off the true heading under the Index = 145°.
7. Finally apply the variation, in this case 2°W. Remember "East is Least, West is Best", the variation is West, hence we add it giving a magnetic heading of 147°.
8. Read the groundspeed below the wind dot – 98 knots.

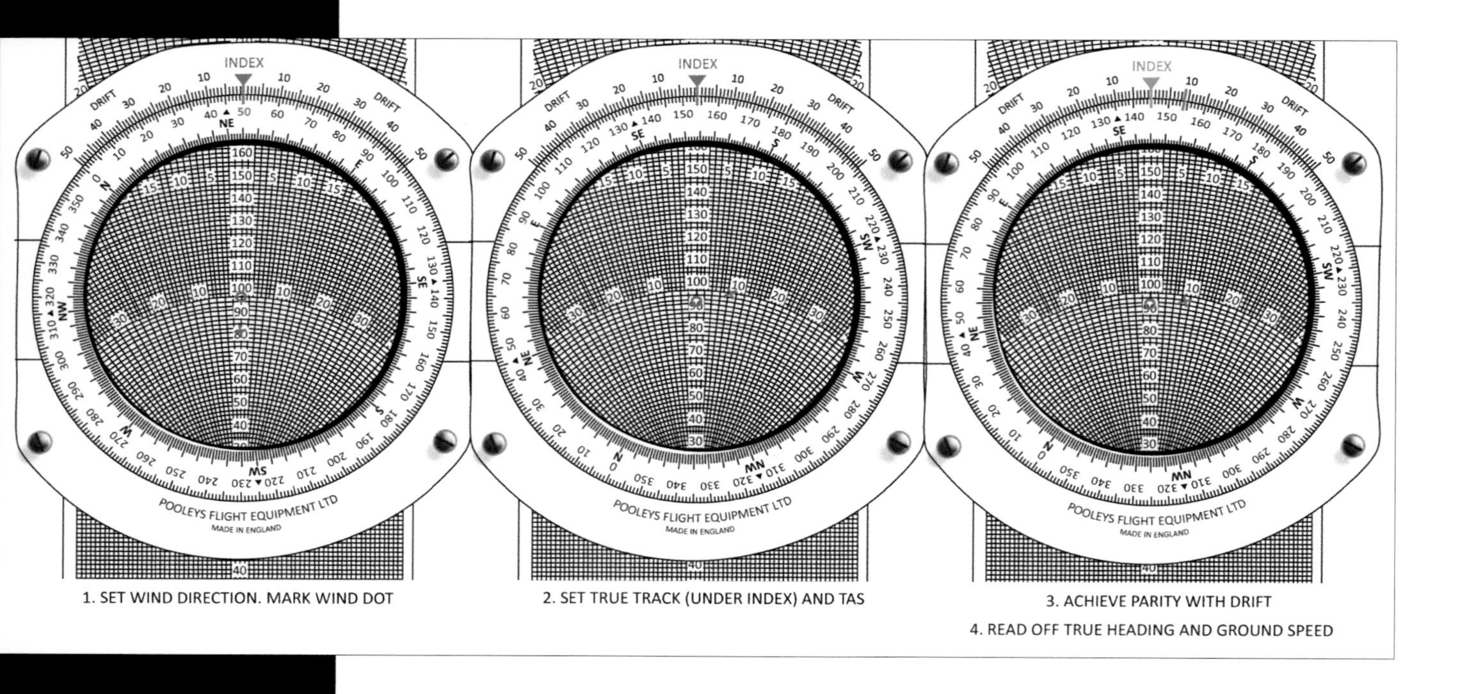

1. SET WIND DIRECTION. MARK WIND DOT

2. SET TRUE TRACK (UNDER INDEX) AND TAS

3. ACHIEVE PARITY WITH DRIFT

4. READ OFF TRUE HEADING AND GROUND SPEED

The CRP can be very easy to misread, drawing a small sketch will give you a rough idea of the answer you expect to obtain to ensure that any amendments are applied correctly.

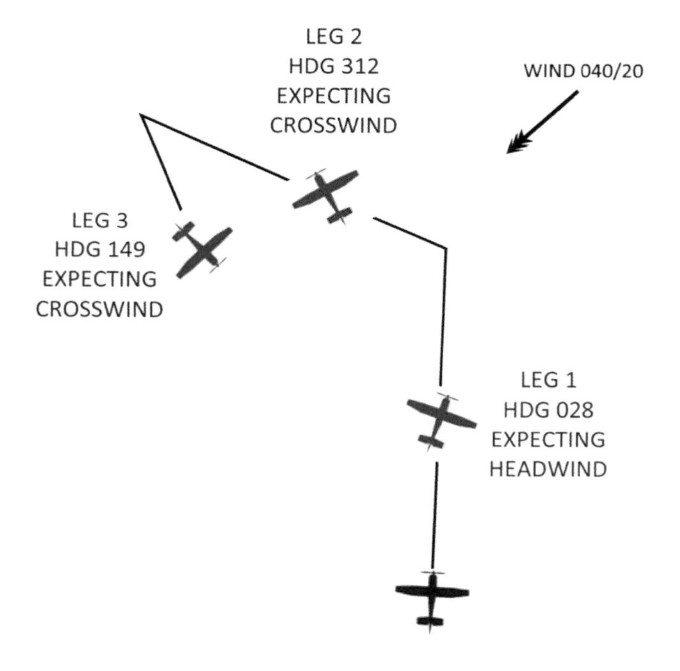

Outer Scale:	Distance	Speed
Inner Scale:	Time	60

To complete the plog calculations, use the front of the CRP to determine the time for each leg.

1. Set the calculated ground speed above the time index.
2. Find the distance for each leg on the outer scale.
3. Read off the time on the inner scale.

END OF PRACTICE PLANNING AND PLOGS

ANSWER SHEETS

NOTE: *Please feel free to photocopying these answer sheet pages when practising tests. All other pages are subject to the copyright law and should not be copied under any circumstances.*

PAPER NO.				
	A	B	C	D
1				
2				
3				
4				
5				
6				
7				
8				
9				
10				
11				
12				
13				
14				
15				
16				
17				
18				
19				
20				

PAPER NO.				
	A	B	C	D
1				
2				
3				
4				
5				
6				
7				
8				
9				
10				
11				
12				
13				
14				
15				
16				
17				
18				
19				
20				

PAPER NO.				
	A	B	C	D
1				
2				
3				
4				
5				
6				
7				
8				
9				
10				
11				
12				
13				
14				
15				
16				
17				
18				
19				
20				

PAPER NO.				
	A	B	C	D
1				
2				
3				
4				
5				
6				
7				
8				
9				
10				
11				
12				
13				
14				
15				
16				
17				
18				
19				
20				

PAPER NO.				
	A	B	C	D
1				
2				
3				
4				
5				
6				
7				
8				
9				
10				
11				
12				
13				
14				
15				
16				
17				
18				
19				
20				

PAPER NO.				
	A	B	C	D
1				
2				
3				
4				
5				
6				
7				
8				
9				
10				
11				
12				
13				
14				
15				
16				
17				
18				
19				
20				

PAPER NO.				
	A	B	C	D
1				
2				
3				
4				
5				
6				
7				
8				
9				
10				
11				
12				
13				
14				
15				
16				
17				
18				
19				
20				

PAPER NO.				
	A	B	C	D
1				
2				
3				
4				
5				
6				
7				
8				
9				
10				
11				
12				
13				
14				
15				
16				
17				
18				
19				
20				

PAPER NO.				
	A	B	C	D
1				
2				
3				
4				
5				
6				
7				
8				
9				
10				
11				
12				
13				
14				
15				
16				
17				
18				
19				
20				

PAPER NO.				
	A	B	C	D
1				
2				
3				
4				
5				
6				
7				
8				
9				
10				
11				
12				
13				
14				
15				
16				
17				
18				
19				
20				

PAPER NO.				
	A	B	C	D
1				
2				
3				
4				
5				
6				
7				
8				
9				
10				
11				
12				
13				
14				
15				
16				
17				
18				
19				
20				

PAPER NO.				
	A	B	C	D
1				
2				
3				
4				
5				
6				
7				
8				
9				
10				
11				
12				
13				
14				
15				
16				
17				
18				
19				
20				